Margaret Sanger

by
Deborah Bachrach

Lucent Books, P.O. Box 289011, San Diego, CA 92198-9011

These and other titles are included in The Importance Of biography series:

Christopher Columbus	Chief Joseph
Marie Curie	Michelangelo
Walt Disney	Richard M. Nixon
Benjamin Franklin	Jackie Robinson
Galileo Galilei	Margaret Sanger
Thomas Jefferson	H.G. Wells

For my grandmothers, Anna Sprafkin and Dora Yellin, whom I never met but whose bravery has greatly influenced my life

Library of Congress Cataloging-in-Publication Data

Bachrach, Deborah, 1943-
    Margaret Sanger / by Deborah Bachrach.
    p. cm.—(Importance of)
    Includes bibliographical references and index.
Summary: A biography of the woman who sacrificed her personal life and health to pioneer safe and legal birth control in the United States and abroad.
    ISBN 1-56006-032-8
    1. Sanger, Margaret, 1879-1966—Juvenile literature. 2. Birth control—United States—Biography—Juvenile literature. 3. Social reformers—United States—Biography—Juvenile literature. 4. Sanger, Margaret, 1879-1966. [1. Social reformers. 2. Feminists. Birth control—History] I. Title. II. Series.
HQ764.S3B33   1993
363.9'6'092—dc20   92-46878
[B]   CIP
                                                              AC

Contents

Foreword

THE IMPORTANCE OF biography series deals with individuals who have made a unique contribution to history. The editors of the series have deliberately chosen to cast a wide net and include people from all fields of endeavor. Individuals from politics, music, art, literature, philosophy, science, sports, and religion are all represented. In addition, the editors did not restrict the series to individuals whose accomplishments have helped change the course of history. Of necessity, this criterion would have eliminated many whose contribution was great, though limited. Charles Darwin, for example, was responsible for radically altering the scientific view of the natural history of the world. His achievements continue to impact the study of science today. Others, such as Chief Joseph of the Nez Percé, played a pivotal role in the history of their own people. While Joseph's influence does not extend much beyond the Nez Percé, his nonviolent resistance to white expansion and his continuing role in protecting his tribe and his homeland remain an inspiration to all.

These biographies are more than factual chronicles. Each volume attempts to emphasize an individual's contributions both in his or her own time and for posterity. For example, the voyages of Christopher Columbus opened the way to European colonization of the New World. Unquestionably, his encounter with the New World brought monumental changes to both Europe and the Americas in his day. Today, however, the broader impact of Columbus's voyages is being critically scrutinized. *Christopher Columbus,* as well as every biography in The Importance Of series, includes and evaluates the most recent scholarship available on each subject.

Each author includes a wide variety of primary and secondary source quotations to document and substantiate his or her work. All quotes are footnoted to show readers exactly how and where biographers derive their information, as well as provide stepping stones to further research. These quotations enliven the text by giving readers eyewitness views of the life and times of each individual covered in The Importance Of series.

Finally, each volume is enhanced by photographs, bibliographies, chronologies, and comprehensive indexes. For both the casual reader and the student engaged in research, The Importance Of biographies will be a fascinating adventure into the lives of people who have helped shape humanity's past, present, and will continue to shape its future.

Important Dates in the Life of Margaret Sanger

President Grant signs Comstock bill into law that bans use of U.S. mail for distribution and information on contraception. — **1873**

1879 — Birth of Margaret Higgins Sanger.

Marriage to William Sanger.

Woman Rebel published; Sanger escapes to Europe and learns about role of physician in birth control. — **1900**

Sanger's involvement with socialist and anarchist groups in New York City.

1910-1912

1914 — Sanger returns to the United States; daughter Peggy dies.

Establishment of first American birth control clinic in Brownsville section of Brooklyn; raid on clinic. — **1915** / **1916** / **1918**

Crane decision rules that physicians can discuss birth control.

First National Birth Control Conference; establishment of American birth control league. — **1922**

1923 — Birth Control Clinical Research Bureau opened in New York City.

International conference in Geneva. — **1927**

1929 — Raid on Clinical Research Bureau.

U.S. vs. One Package authorizes mail for use for medically used contraceptives. — **1936**

Eleanor Roosevelt declares support for birth control.

1940

Establishment of Planned Parenthood Federation of America unifies various birth control organizations. — **1942**

Stockholm conference on sex education.

1946

Research at Worcester Laboratory begins on the "pill"; International Planned Parenthood Federation founded. — **1952**

Draper Report on necessity of population planning in foreign aid rejected by President Dwight Eisenhower.

1959

1960

"Pill" released for general use. — **1965**

Griswold vs. Connecticut determines that an individual has a right to federally guaranteed privacy.

Death of Margaret Sanger on September 6. — **1966**

A Woman with a Cause

Margaret Sanger was a pioneer in opening the public discussion of birth control and in developing safe, affordable contraceptive devices in the United States. When she undertook what she viewed as a crusade to liberate women from the tragedy of unwanted pregnancies, she trod upon many of the most strongly held views of the majority of people in the United States. Religious and civic leaders, women's groups, and the law all believed that interference with the natural process of conception and birth was immoral, unpatriotic, or illegal.

Nevertheless, Margaret Sanger found the strength to combat these forces. One by one she took them on. She overcame enormous obstacles and in the end achieved her objectives and changed the lives of millions of women throughout the world.

Such perseverance requires unusual fortitude. Several factors in her upbringing contributed to Sanger's strength to continue the fight to develop and distribute readily available means of contraception. First, she had suffered many privations in her childhood. Second, she was heavily influenced by her strong father's unconventional social, political, and religious attitudes.

As a result of her upbringing, Sanger became determined to alter the social forces that she believed helped to impoverish her early years. Her determination led her to take chances that other people feared to attempt.

Each success made her still more determined to persevere. But her fifty-year

Margaret Sanger devoted her life to freeing women from unwanted pregnancy. She succeeded, in large part, through single-minded determination.

Sanger had many prominent friends, including American actor Otis Skinner (left) and British writer H.G. Wells (right).

struggle on behalf of women's contraceptive freedom often blinded Sanger to the needs of those closest to her. She frequently ignored the pleadings for attention from her husbands, her children, her siblings, and her closest and most devoted associates as she pursued national and international objectives. As biographer Lawrence Lader relates:

> Her work had become an obsession that was to rule out the strongest ties in life, sometimes even her children. Much as she loved Stuart, Grant and Peggy, the misery, the need of a million other mothers and children now drove her onward as if she had become the single voice of all their hopes.[1]

She grew increasingly ruthless in her tactics as obstacles placed in her path made waging her battle more dangerous,

as well as financially and personally costly. In the process she discounted the contributions of other people involved in the birth control movement. She became selfish, claiming full credit for victories won along the way with the help of numerous faithful followers. She used people for political or financial assistance and then discarded them. In addition she was a terrible administrator with poor financial judgment. At best she had an uneven understanding of how the American political system worked.

Her personal life became increasingly disordered over the years. She frequently left her children with virtual strangers for long periods of time while she went on speaking tours. Abroad, she became romantically involved with many prominent men who could be of assistance to her in the birth control movement. She may have married her second husband for his social position and for the wealth he could contribute to her crusade. Then, while she spent his money on the birth control movement, she lived her life almost completely apart from him while she continued her numerous amorous pursuits all over the world.

Nor did she take care of her own person. Through a lifetime of campaigning, Margaret Sanger largely ignored the care of her frail, tubercular body. She suffered several heart attacks and did not rest long enough to fully recover. As a result, toward the end of her life, she became highly dependent upon alcohol and various narcotics to shield her from pain and to artificially maintain her waning strength. She was determined to live to see the comple-

tion of the development of the birth control pill.

The public knew almost nothing of this personal, dark side of Margaret Sanger's life. She deliberately concealed these private matters. She understood all too well that she had to maintain the outer appearance of a demure, soft-spoken, earnest crusader, a devoted wife and mother, if she were to overcome the enormous obstacles confronting the American birth control movement. Mere whispers of open sexual attitudes, for example, would have provided the Roman Catholic church with sufficient ammunition to discredit the woman the church viewed as one of its most dangerous American enemies.

So Margaret Sanger, like any animal

A Social Radical

Margaret Sanger believed that women of her time were enslaved by pregnancy and childbirth. In her book, Woman and the New Race, *she wrote:*

"The most far-reaching social development of modern times is the revolt of woman against sex servitude. The most important force in the remaking of the world is a free motherhood. Beside this force, the elaborate international programmes of modern statesmen are weak and superficial. Diplomats may formulate leagues of nations and nations may pledge their utmost strength to maintain them, statesmen may dream of reconstructing the world out of alliances, hegemonies and spheres of influence, but woman, continuing to produce explosive populations, will convert these pledges into the proverbial scraps of paper; or she may, by controlling birth, lift motherhood to the plane of a voluntary, intelligent function, and remake the world. When the world is thus remade, it will exceed the dream of statesman, reformer and revolutionist.

A 1916 portrait of Sanger and sons Grant and Stuart. Sanger's obsession with her work often kept her from her children.

in perusing these papers, scholars have discovered the other, less attractive, less acceptable side of the great, but ruthless, egotistical, selfish, and self-centered social crusader. Several of them have tried to provide what are considered to be more balanced evaluations of Margaret Sanger.

These recent works offer the reader additional information about Sanger's personal life. They do not, however, significantly alter the facts regarding her immensely single-minded and ultimately successful fight on behalf of women's contraceptive freedom.

This book emphasizes the enormous contribution to society Margaret Higgins Sanger made, rather than the unconventional aspects of her personal life. Therefore, it largely disregards what would have been considered her darker side by her own contemporaries and by the social mores of her era. Since she succeeded in large part because of her ability to maintain a suitable public image, it is historically accurate to present an account of her contribution to women and to society from this perspective. Many of her contemporaries saw her as an undaunted David figure, taking on the Goliath of society's rigid control over women's reproductive freedom. While this picture is somewhat exaggerated, it is important to understand her contributions within Sanger's own historical context. It is only by focusing on her professional accomplishments that readers can understand Margaret Sanger's achievements.

using camouflage for safety, adopted a public appearance suitable for a woman taking on one of the most incendiary social causes of the first half of the twentieth century. And she deliberately worked to enhance that false image through her various writings, especially her *Autobiography*.

She did not, however, intend for her personal life to remain a secret forever. She left a voluminous collection of diaries, letters, and other written materials to the library of Smith College and the Library of Congress in Washington, D.C., where they are available to researchers. Recently,

Chapter

1 Beginnings and Stirrings

Let God and Man decree
Laws for themselves and not for me:
Their deeds I judge and much
*   condemn*
Yet when did I make laws for them?

—A.E. Houseman

Margaret Higgins Sanger was born in 1879 in the grim, smoky factory town of Corning, New York, which is located on the banks of the Chemung River. She was the fourth daughter and sixth surviving child of Michael Hennessy Higgins and Anne Purcell Higgins.

The Higgins family was extremely poor. The children wore old, shabby clothing and were sometimes teased by the other town children because of their appearance. They were often hungry and shivered from the cold of the New York winters because there seldom was enough money to buy sufficient food and coal.

The family's poverty was due in large part to the fact that Margaret's father, although a talented stonecutter, held radical social views that made him a relative outcast in their small Catholic community. He took an ardent interest in local politics and spent as much time arguing about social theory as he did supporting his growing family. As a result, Margaret and her sisters and brothers had their minds filled

with their father's ideas about liberalizing late nineteenth-century American society.

For example, Michael Higgins felt strongly that organized religion interfered with the freedom of people to live their

The Higgins sisters: Ethel, Margaret, Nan, and Mary. The family was quite poor and the children were often cold and hungry.

Michael Higgins (left) demonstrates a new stonecutting technique. His outspoken views on the Catholic church cost him his job as the Catholic cemetery's gravestone cutter.

own lives. Although Mrs. Higgins was a Catholic, Mr. Higgins was an atheist, a person who does not believe in the existence of God. As a result, the Higgins children were raised without much religious instruction. They particularly hated the Catholic church because of the priests' frequent threats to revoke their support of Michael Higgins as gravestone cutter for the Catholic cemetery unless he kept his nonconforming religious views to himself.

Michael Higgins held as unconventional views on male and female roles as on religion. He believed in equality between the sexes. Women as well as men should read and argue about social theories in order to understand the forces that controlled their lives, he argued. He was particularly supportive of the work of Susan B. Anthony, the early American feminist who founded the National Woman Suffrage Association in 1869.

He also believed that all class distinctions between rich and poor should be eliminated. To achieve this end, Higgins argued for the abolishment of private property. In particular, Mr. Higgins held that land ownership widened the gulf between rich and poor, and he felt this to be one of the gravest social injustices. Few people in the working class town of Corning, New York, were interested in the social radicalism that fired Higgins's imagination and later that of his young daughter, Margaret.

Nevertheless, Michael Higgins made no secret of his unpopular views. He discussed them in the town's taverns and at public meetings and shared them with his many children. Once, showing a good deal of insight, he announced to his large brood that "The one thing I've been able to give you is a free mind. Use it well and give something back to your generation." [2]

The Higgins children were taunted by their neighbors because of their father's outspoken views and their absence from church. In the Catholic community in which they lived, the Higgins brood was considered to be the devil's children. This ostracism made some of the Higgins children strong. It also made most of them turn away from religion entirely.

Corningitis

Margaret Sanger often said that all of her problems arose from the fact that she suffered from Corningitis, having been raised in Corning, New York. But her niece, Olive Byrne Richard, said that the Sangers' shared Irish heritage was to blame for their problems. In a letter to her aunt, excerpted from Madeline Gray's biography of Sanger, she presented this view:

"I also was afflicted at one time with Corningitis, an affliction I shared with you until I found out that poor old Corning was not to blame, except that what we felt was first experienced there. Actually, it was Irish fear. All the Irish feel it inherently and they seem to embrace any religion or way of life that nourishes it, because fear is thrilling to them. They are afraid to live; afraid to die. They laugh a lot because they are afraid they will cry. They usually die of a fearsome illness and go a fearful place. I still find it hard at times to be reasonable about it.

But all the Higgins girls did something about it. Mary to soothe the fearsome path of the people she loved; Nan eventually to say, 'I will be bigger than it is' and to help others to be so; Ethel to run away from it; and you to say, 'What is the biggest fear there is? I will fight it!' In your experience, your mother's fear of pregnancy was the biggest. You found it possible to project your fear into the world that it might be united with a common fear and form a Goliath worth slaying. Actually, when you travel through Corning, you should wake up laughing and with a thumb at nose."

Her Father's Influence

Of all his children, Margaret listened most closely to her father's advice. As a child she sat, spellbound, as her small, powerfully built, red-headed father thumped the bare kitchen table to emphasize the latest social theories. Margaret adored her father. She often watched as he carved his beautiful headstones, and she accompanied him when he went to speak at political gatherings.

She knew that her father was willing to defend his views with his life. Once, Margaret was with Mr. Higgins when a mob of workers threatened to attack him. Higgins had invited a social radical named Robert Ingersoll to Corning. The talk was to be given at the small Catholic church, the only building in town large enough to hold all the people who came to hear him—or to taunt him.

Many townspeople were infuriated with Higgins because he tried to have Ingersoll speak in the church. As the yelling crowd threatened Higgins, he held his ground against them and defended the right of freedom of speech. Years later Margaret also confronted angry mobs trying to stop her from presenting unpopular views. The memory of her father's courage in confronting the angry men of Corning no doubt gave her strength to stand up to the fury of her own opponents.

But Margaret also knew the price her father paid for expressing his beliefs. The Catholic community in Corning eventually boycotted Higgins and no one would buy his beautifully cut gravestones. Margaret waved goodbye as Michael Higgins would tramp away to find work in distant towns.

Clearly, Margaret imitated her father's rebellious nature. All her life the small and frail woman was never afraid to state her opinion. Once she decided on a course of action, she never looked back.

Although exhausted and weakened by tuberculosis, Margaret's mother, Anne Purcell Higgins, cared for her children most of her married life.

Her Mother's Fate as Inspiration

Much as Michael Higgins affected her life, Margaret was equally influenced by the hard life and early death of her mother, Anne. Mrs. Higgins suffered from tuberculosis. But the family was far too poor to afford the medical care and rest she needed. Although constantly tired and weak from disease, Anne Higgins continued to conceive, bear, nurse, and care for children for most of her married life.

Margaret was very aware of her family's difficulties. She helped her mother care for her younger brothers and sisters because Margaret's two oldest sisters, Nan and Mary, had already left home to work outside the family, one as a domestic and the other in a factory.

These older sisters wanted Margaret to continue her education after she completed grammar school. Nan and Mary generously contributed money from their meager earnings to enable Margaret to attend a private school after she graduated from eighth grade. The preparatory school was called Claverack College and it was located near the town of Hudson in the Catskill Mountains of New York state. Margaret herself also helped pay for her schooling by doing laundry and waiting on dormitory tables at the school.

Margaret hoped to become a doctor. She wished to go on to the Cornell University School of Medicine once she graduated from Claverack. But her dreams of medical school were shattered two years later when her father called her home to care for her mother during the last tragic months of Anne Higgins's life. At age sixteen, Margaret nursed her mother and once again cared for the younger Higgins children. She also contracted tuberculosis from her dying mother. Margaret would be affected by the disease at various times throughout the rest of her life. During this time at home, Margaret thought a great deal about her mother's difficult, frustrating life.

Her mother had been pregnant a total of eighteen times. The number was not unusual for women of her social class. As Margaret witnessed the slow deterioration of her mother, she became determined to

Sanger at age fourteen, two years before her mother's death.

devote her life to improving other women's lives. She knew that her mother and her neighbors lived in dreary circumstances. Their days were filled with the care of many children and with unfulfilled dreams. They never had an opportunity to get an education, to live independent lives, or to experience some of life's comforts. In her mind Margaret associated poverty with the large families so common in her childhood neighborhood. Margaret also understood that women like her mother gave birth to additional children year after year regardless of whether they had the money or strength to care for them.

Margaret believed that there was something terribly unfair about these facts. She also knew she did not want such circumstances to determine her own fate. So, instead of settling down with a local boy who wanted to marry her, six months after her mother died in 1896, Margaret Sanger left home. She knew that her dreams of becoming a doctor were now remote—poverty had made a lengthy college education virtually impossible. But she also knew that she could not live in the limited, hopeless world of the women of Corning, New York.

A Nursing Career

Instead, Margaret became a nursing student in White Plains Hospital in Westchester County, New York. She knew that as a nurse she would be able to earn her own living. She believed that financial independence, resulting from a useful profession, would be necessary if she were to be able to choose the kind of life she wanted.

The time she spent as a nursing probationer was exhausting and exciting. Her days were long, the equipment she used was outdated, and the work was hard. In the process Margaret learned something about the delivery and care of newborns. In her *Autobiography*, published in 1938, she describes how she sometimes was sent out on cases and found herself entirely in charge of a delivery.

> Often I was called in the middle of the night on a maternity case, perhaps ten miles away from the hospital, where I had to sterilize the water and boil the forceps over a wood fire in the kitchen stove while the doctor scrubbed up as best he could. Many times labor terminated before he could arrive and I had to perform the delivery myself.[3]

Frequently her patients asked Margaret for information to help them stop having additional children. Unfortunately, Margaret could only turn them away. As she wrote: "I was at a loss to answer their intimate questions, and passed them along to the doctor, who more often than not snorted, 'She ought to be ashamed of herself to talk to a young girl about things like that.'"[4] Little information on this subject was available in the United States in the early years of the twentieth century. In fact, it was illegal to publish the little information that was available.

Margaret Meets William Sanger

While her professional career took shape, Margaret's personal life also blossomed. Margaret's life changed dramatically and happily when she was nineteen: she met William Sanger at a dance held for the nursing students. William Sanger was an architect, ten years her senior. Since a nursing student was forbidden to marry, the two secretly wed during one of Margaret's lunch hours. They managed to keep the secret until Margaret completed her year of nursing training.

In the following ten years the Sangers had three children, Stuart, Grant, and Peggy. They built and were burned out of a beautiful home along the Hudson River and then moved to New York City. William Sanger worked as an architect and dreamed of becoming an artist. Margaret Sanger eventually resumed her nursing career in 1911 to help out with the family finances. "I eventually took special obstetri-

As her dreams of becoming a doctor faded, Sanger set her sights on a career as a nurse.

Sanger and her six-week-old son Grant in 1906. After a secret wedding, Sanger and her husband William had two sons and a daughter.

cal and surgical cases assigned to me," [5] she wrote.

In her *Autobiography* Sanger describes how she was able to balance work and family life:

> During these years in New York trained nurses were in great demand. Few people wanted to enter hospitals; they were afraid they might be "practiced" upon, and consented to go only in desperate emergencies. Sentiment was especially vehement in the matter of having babies. A woman's own bedroom, no matter how inconveniently arranged, was the usual place for her lying-in. I was not sufficiently free from domestic duties to be a general nurse, but I could ordinarily manage obstetrical cases because I was notified far enough ahead to plan my schedule. And after serving my two weeks I could get home again. [6]

Margaret's return to the field of nursing brought her face to face with the stark realities of life and death among the poor women and children who lived in the crowded tenement buildings on the Lower East Side of New York City. The Visiting Nurses Association and the Henry Street Settlement House sent out nurses like

Sanger's work delivering babies in the crowded tenement buildings on the Lower East Side of New York City provided her with a view of the stark lives impoverished women led.

Margaret to assist in the home deliveries of the poorest of poor women. What she saw in those hellholes horrified her. The sights of suffering and poverty combined in her mind with bittersweet memories of her own mother. These experiences slowly turned Margaret Sanger from a sympathetic woman into a fierce and determined warrior on behalf of the right of women to control their reproductive lives.

She ascribed women's terrible living conditions to the evil of male dominance and ambition. She believed that women's role of producing children fueled these ambitions by providing additional factory workers and soldiers. Sanger insisted that, until women gained control of their own reproductive systems, they would never be free to live productive, fulfilling lives. As she wrote in her *Autobiography*:

> No system of society depending for its continuation on intelligent humans can stand long unless it encourages the control of the birth rate and includes contraceptive knowledge as a right.[7]

Once she had embarked on her crusade, Sanger never questioned the correctness of her cause.

Political Activism

At the same time that Margaret was experiencing firsthand the dire poverty of the slums, she also became increasingly politically active. Her husband William belonged to the Socialist political party. Margaret joined also. William Sanger believed that the enactment of socialist legislation would demonstrate America's commitment to the working class in society. Margaret was enthralled by the excitement of the socialist movement and by the clever, dedicated, and fascinating people who spread its gospel.

She received a broad education in social and political theory from the many guests who visited the Sangers. Their home became a gathering place for artists, writers, and social revolutionaries. Margaret Sanger listened carefully to their points of view.

These people were angry with the inequalities that existed in American society in the early twentieth century. They deplored the long hours the poor were forced to work and the horrible conditions in the factories and mines that made the lives of lower-class workers painful and short. They denounced the absence of child labor laws, the absence of health insurance, and the absence of the vote for women.

The Sangers and their friends believed that the captains of industry, like the Rockefellers, had made their fortunes by overworking and underpaying working people. They were exploiters and their property should be seized and redistributed according to the more radical socialist thought of the times.

Many of these young intellectuals were communists. In addition to their extremely liberal political views, they also espoused radical social theories. For example, many of them believed in free love and, there-

Children in a poor New York City neighborhood find relief in the cooling spray of a fire hydrant. Living conditions in neighborhoods such as these spurred Sanger to action.

fore, did not see the value of marriage and traditional family life. The Sangers' friends—feminists and anarchists like Emma Goldman, socialists like Bill Haywood, revolutionaries like journalist John Reed, and intellectuals and philosophers such as Will Durant and Walter Lippmann—all believed that massive changes would have to take place before social and economic equality existed in modern society.

Margaret thrived on these radical ideas. She soon became more politically active than her husband and was frequently away from home at various committee meetings. She did not like staying home and tending to the needs of her family. The rich intellectual environment in which she lived seemed to offer an opportunity to expand her horizons and make her life more exciting and rewarding. Margaret's dedication to this movement eventually led to a separation from her husband in 1914.

In the meantime Margaret began to join her new friends in protest marches against unfair labor conditions. The protesters wanted to establish the right of workers to join and organize labor unions, the right of women to equal pay for equal work, and the right for all people to a decent standard of living. As she worked to assist in the fight for social equality, Margaret was reminded of her father's concern for social justice, of her mother's pain, and of her own cold and hungry childhood in Corning.

A Strike Crystallizes Margaret's Mission

All of these memories and impressions came into clear focus for Margaret in 1912. In that year the labor movement in the United States became increasingly violent. In the wake of a nationwide depression, many factory owners tried to cut still further into the already low living stan-

Like her friends Emma Goldman (left) and Walter Lippmann (right), Sanger believed that social and economic equality could only be achieved through massive change.

A Troubled Marriage

As Margaret Sanger became involved in the socialist movement she began to pull further away from her husband. In the following letter from William Sanger to his wife, excerpted from Madeline Gray's book, he expresses his love and his sadness at what has happened to their marriage.

"Personalities are crowding around you, and if you follow the anarchist teaching, it would mean you must know these personalities in all relations. Well, I have not yet adapted myself to this.

Sometime I wonder whether I am not too constant and appear to narrow your life to knowing completely only one personality. But this I shall express again and again—that to be alone linked with your life is the jewel of my inspiration. You speak, dear love, that in our life together you have given me the best and deepest love—yes, and I have felt it—that you were the only woman who ever cared to understand me.

But you have advanced sexually—you once said that you need to be in different relations [with men] as a service for the women of your time. To all this I have no answer."

dard of working people. In response, a labor organization called the International Workers of the World, better known as the IWW, called for a strike against the Lawrence, Massachusetts, textile mills. The IWW included women in its union and even gave some of them responsible jobs. Margaret was attracted by the excitement and the equality the radical movement offered. She became involved in the dispute.

When the labor conflict became ugly and violent, strike supporters tried to find safe, temporary homes for the strikers' children in New York City. Margaret Sanger was stirred by the ferocity of the Lawrence strike and by the plight of the strikers' children. She threw herself into the very center of activity by helping to

Members of the IWW face off against armed state militia during the textile mills strike in Lawrence, Massachusetts.

Children of striking textile workers march down Fifth Avenue in New York City bearing placards denouncing the actions of their parents' employers.

care for the children sent to New York City for safety.

She was struck by the dire condition of these little evacuees. Almost all the children were emaciated and had enlarged tonsils and adenoids which betrayed untreated medical conditions of long standing. Even though it was winter, only 4 out of the 119 children in her charge had underwear, only 20 wore coats, and none wore woolen clothing. The deplorable condition of these children underscored the heartlessness of the society Margaret and her radical friends denounced.

At the end of the strike the lone Socialist member of the U. S. House of Representatives wanted to hear details about what had happened in Lawrence. Because of her nursing training, Margaret Sanger was selected to testify on behalf of the children of Lawrence before a congressional subcommittee in Washington, D.C. There she expressed political views that were as revolutionary as those of her new circle of friends.

During her congressional testimony it became clear that Margaret Sanger's social and political theories had developed a new coherence and maturity. She was beginning to make a connection between overpopulation, the inhumane response of society to the needs of women and children, and the lack of birth control information. She was on the threshhold of a career that would revolutionize the lives of women in the United States. That career would also result in the creation of greater social possibilities for women the world over.

Chapter

2 Women and Reproductive Choices

There is no force in the world so great as that of an idea when its hour has struck.
—Victor Hugo

Margaret Sanger faced enormous obstacles as she embarked on her career as a social reformer on behalf of women's repro-

Women's fashion reflected the Puritan ideas common during Sanger's childhood. Gloved hands, long sleeves, high necks, and ankle-length hemlines left only facial skin showing.

ductive freedom. She would have to possess enormous personal courage and an iron will to bring about radical changes in society's views on sexual matters. These views were firmly entrenched and sanctioned by men, religion, and the overwhelming majority of the medical profession.

When Margaret Sanger was born, people simply did not openly discuss reproduction. They did not discuss birth control. In fact, polite society did not even discuss body parts. Legs were referred to as limbs and even the "limbs" of furniture were covered by fabric.

In this prudish world dominated by Puritan ideas, the entire subject of sex was taboo. Young ladies were supposed to know nothing about it, and young men snickered about it when young ladies were not present. Even married couples frequently knew little about the subject.

The Comstock Law

In such a restrictive social environment the entire subject of contraception—preventing fertilization or implantation of the egg—was never discussed. In fact, toward the end of the nineteenth century, the en-

Anthony Comstock believed contraception led to prostitution and that contraceptive information and devices were akin to pornography.

tire subject came under the jurisdiction of federal and state law. The Comstock Law, passed in 1873, equated contraception with pornography. As a result, both were subject to the same restrictions and legal penalties.

The law dealing with contraception was named after its chief promoter, Anthony Comstock. Comstock was secretary to the New York Society for the Prevention of Vice. He was a deeply religious man who felt that he worked in the service of God. Comstock held especially fervent views on the subject of contraception. He believed contraception led to prostitution. When married couples abstained from sex as a means of contraception, for example, Comstock believed that men were likely to visit prostitutes. Therefore, in Comstock's

view, the subject of contraception was "obscene, lewd, lascivious, filthy and indecent."[8]

Under Comstock's influence many Americans also came to view contraceptive information and contraceptive devices as pornographic. The importation of pornography and its distribution through the U.S. mail had long been illegal. Comstock and his supporters wanted to add contraceptive information to the list of obscene things that could not be imported into the United States.

He converted many people to his point of view. Many legislators in Congress supported his bill because they believed it would protect the sexual purity of Americans and that it would reduce the number of quack remedies for contraception that were advertised in many newspapers. President Ulysses S. Grant signed the Comstock bill into law on March 3, 1873. It became illegal to mail, transport, or import into the United States any kind of birth control information or devices. Violations of the law would result in the imposition of harsh penalties.

Twenty-two states soon followed the lead of the federal government in the area of contraceptive information. Some of the state legislatures enacted into law even more stringent bills than the federal laws that forbade the publication or distribution of information regarding contraceptive devices.

One writer noted that the Comstock Law and the state "little Comstock laws" represented an example of "the codification of Puritan attitudes into statute law." Another said that "many people were more concerned about the moral effects of knowledge than about the medical effects of ignorance."[9]

Anyone found guilty of violating the Comstock Law could be imprisoned. Comstock himself, upon request, was appointed as a special agent of the United States Postal Service for New York so that he could see that the antipornography and anticontraception laws were fully enforced in his own state.

Through Comstock's vigilance, several physicians were found guilty of violating the Comstock Law. These physicians were entrapped by Comstock and his female agents. The agents, acting as patients, sent letters to these physicians requesting written confirmation of the information they had received during recent office visits. Since the physicians had provided information regarding contraceptive methods to people they believed to be married female patients, they complied with these requests.

Under the Comstock Law, this action was illegal. These physicians were prosecuted and sentenced to varying prison terms. One received a ten-year sentence at hard labor for discussing contraceptive matters within his own practice. These

President Theodore Roosevelt viewed contraception as unpatriotic and so became a forceful advocate for the Comstock Law.

penalties quickly became well-known throughout the profession. Their severity was sufficient to dissuade the American medical profession from actively exploring advances in the area of contraception and family planning.

It would have been foolhardy for physicians to have challenged the Comstock Law in the late nineteenth century. Federal and state laws were not alone in opposing the distribution of such information and services. Major religious organizations condemned it as well. Virtually all organized religions, spearheaded by the Roman Catholic church, had strong reservations regarding any unnatural interference in conception and birth and with ideas regarding family planning.

The law and religious groups received the hearty, shrill support of President Theodore Roosevelt. He believed that a strong America required a large and grow-

A 1915 cartoon deftly criticizes Comstock's views.

"Your Honor, this woman gave birth to a naked child!"

ing population to compete in the world. Roosevelt, then, believed contraception was simply unpatriotic. And he never lost an opportunity to roar out his opposition to those who advocated small families: "If America aspires to ascendancy in world affairs American parents must breed large families."[10]

Available Birth Control Methods

Despite all these legal, professional, religious, and social obstacles, American women had a great need and desire for contraception information. Some basic information had been available for a long time. For example, men had long had access to condoms made of animal intestines. They were popularly known as condoms after a Dr. Condom introduced sheaths made of sheep guts into the court of King Charles II of England in the late seventeenth century. Rather than preventing conception, however, these sheaths were used to prevent sexually transmitted diseases such as gonorrhea and syphilis. With the development of vulcanized rubber late in the nineteenth century, condom production became more effective, but still they were primarily used to preserve men's health. Even with the introduction of a more comfortable material, latex, in the 1930s, condoms were not seen as an effective birth control technology.

Upper-class women had access to other methods. They were able to obtain chemicals such as sulfate of zinc to kill sperm and prevent conception. Items such as beeswax disks were used to keep sperm from entering the uterus. Some

Mrs. Poor Patient:—"If you're rich, the law don't count"

Despite the Comstock Law, wealthy women had access to birth control. A 1918 cartoon comments on this inequity.

women used sponges moistened with lemon juice as a spermicide. Even some primitive diaphragms, known as "Dutch cups," were available to prevent conception.

It was illegal, of course, to obtain most contraceptive items, except for condoms. Women bought their supplies in secret from special sources and never discussed their use outside a very close circle of friends. They feared that their suppliers might be arrested.

These early contraceptive methods were also very expensive. So the knowledge of their existence and their availability was limited to those who were well-to-do. They were, however, fairly effective in helping to limit the size of upper- and middle-class families. And keeping down family size was socially and religiously acceptable to the more affluent women in American society.

Poor people had little or no choice in the matter of how many children they were to have. Contraception was virtually unknown to them. And even if they had known that contraception was possible, they had never had a spokesperson to suggest that they could or should have control over their own bodies.

Pregnancy and Poverty

Margaret Sanger was among the earliest to make this suggestion. Her opportunity occurred while she worked as a nurse in New York. As Margaret Sanger worked with immigrant families, she found that the more children women had, the poorer they were, and the worse was their health and that of their offspring.

Her firsthand experiences in the large, airless tenements, terribly crowded and lacking in adequate toilet facilities and running water, dramatically brought home to her the connection between large families and poverty and disease. All this merely reinforced what she had seen among the young children of Lawrence, Massachusetts.

On one block alone of the area where Sanger worked—bordered by Canal, Hester, Eldridge, and Forsythe streets—3,000 people lived, including 450 babies. There was one bathtub for all of these people in the backyard of one of the tenements. In the tenth ward of the city there was a total of 76,000 people crowded into 1,174 tene-

A child gets a bath in a tenement building in 1905. The airless, crowded tenement buildings rarely had adequate toilet facilities or running water.

Abortion Mills

When Margaret Sanger worked as a nurse on New York's Lower East Side, she saw women lining up to have abortions. She describes one such ghastly scene in her book, My Fight for Birth Control:

"In this atmosphere abortions and births became the main theme of conversation. On Saturday nights I have seen groups of fifty to one hundred women going into questionable offices well known in the community for cheap abortions. A quick examination, a probe inserted into the uterus, turned a few times to disturb the fertilized ovum, and then the woman was sent home. Usually the flow began the next day and often continued four or five weeks. Sometimes an ambulance carried the victim to the hospital for a curettage, and if she returned home at all she was looked upon as a lucky woman.

The menace of another pregnancy hung like a sword over the head of every poor woman I came in contact with that year."

ment buildings.

Almost all the poor, uneducated immigrant families with whom she worked shared the same sad story. Italians, Jews, Poles, and Irish all produced large families. Often twelve children and their parents crowded together in three rooms, and the father was unable to feed and clothe them all. Boarders also lived with these families in their tiny apartments. These single men were taken in to supplement the immigrant family's meager earnings.

Margaret Sanger came to believe that a large proportion of the misery of these people could be relieved through the limitation of family size. She discovered that, in spite of religious teachings to the contrary, many of her poor patients were desperate to keep down the number of their children for economic reasons. For others, preventing the birth of another child

was a matter of life and death. Since they had no contraceptive devices available to them, these mothers had to resort to another, illegal method of family control—abortion.

Sanger wrote that "On Saturday night I have seen groups of fifty to one hundred women going into questionable offices, well known in the community for cheap abortions."[11] For these women, further complications lay ahead. Some would hemorrhage and die from infections and internal damage resulting from surgery conducted under unsanitary, inhumane conditions. Those who died left luckless children who often could not fend for themselves. These children of poverty and squalor also were doomed to lives of privation and desperation.

Other women, Margaret Sanger discovered, tried to abort themselves. They used whatever means they had available to destroy the fetuses whose conceptions they could not prevent. They swallowed ground glass, drops of turpentine on sugar cubes, lye, and other deadly liquids. They believed that by swallowing these dangerous substances they would cause internal bleeding and a shock to their systems which, in turn, would cause spontaneous abortion.

Others tried to abort themselves by inserting knitting needles, shoe hooks, and other sharp items into their uteruses. Any instrument would do in hopes of bringing on the terrible cramps and severe bleeding that meant the fetus had been aborted. Still others tried throwing themselves down flights of stairs. Some women committed suicide rather than undergo the birth of yet another unwanted child. It was estimated by social workers and hospital authorities that these various methods produced about 100,000 abortions in New York City alone in 1912.

Sadie Sachs

Margaret Sanger was particularly affected by the fate of one of her patients, a woman named Sadie Sachs. Margaret cared for Mrs. Sachs after a self-induced abortion. Mrs. Sachs then begged her doctor to help her prevent an additional pregnancy, which her doctor agreed might cause her death.

The physician's only advice was "Tell Mr. Sachs to sleep on the roof." Abstinence from intercourse was all Mrs. Sachs's physician could recommend to prevent pregnancy. Several months later Sadie Sachs

Sanger found that many poor families desperately wanted to limit their family size to keep their children from lives of despair. This proved difficult without access to birth control.

died in Margaret Sanger's arms. Sadie was a victim of septicemia, resulting from yet another self-induced abortion.

Margaret Sanger described her sadness and outrage after the senseless death of Mrs. Sachs. She wandered the streets in a daze. And then she came to a major decision.

> I resolved that women should have knowledge of contraception. They have every right to know about their own bodies. I would strike out. I would scream from the housetops. I would tell the world what was going on in the lives of these poor women. I would be heard. No matter what it should cost, I would be heard.[12]

Mrs. Sachs's death crystallized the direction in which Margaret would move.

Sanger was opposed to abortion as a primary means of birth control and, indeed, throughout her career she did not respond to inquiries on the subject. The root of the evil, she believed, was not abortion in American society. Instead, it was the unavailability of inexpensive contraceptive information for the poor masses of women. Margaret Sanger set out on a dangerous, lonely crusade to bring women that information.

The Call

On November 17, 1912, Margaret Sanger published the first of a series of outspoken articles for a Socialist monthly called *The Call*. The articles appeared under the title

A poor tenement family sits working around a table. Sanger felt that the large sizes of poor families contributed to their economic situation.

Sanger's Sense of Helplessness Leads to Action

In her Autobiography, *Margaret Sanger explained her anger at a social system that permitted women to die needlessly because of the absence of birth control techniques. The following selection shows her feelings at the time of the death of one of her patients:*

"After I left that desolate house I walked and walked and walked; for hours and hours I kept on, bag in hand, thinking, regretting, dreading to stop; fearful of my conscience, dreading to face my own accusing soul. At three in the morning I arrived home. . . .

As I stood at the window and looked out, the miseries and problems of that sleeping city arose before me in a clear vision like a panorama: crowded homes; too many children; babies dying in infancy; mothers overworked. . . . Half sick most of their lives . . . made into drudges; children working in cellars; children aged six and seven pushed into the labor market to help earn a living; another baby on the way; still another; yet another.

I was now finished with superficial cures, with doctors and nurses and social workers who were brought face to face with this overwhelming truth of women's needs and yet turned to pass on the other side. They must be made to see the facts. I resolved that women should have knowledge of contraception. They have every right to know about their own bodies. I would strike out. I would scream from the housetops. I would tell the world what was going on in the lives of these poor women. I would be heard. No matter what it should cost. I would be heard."

"What Every Girl Should Know." They discussed basic public health issues as they related to girls and women. They talked about the basic physiological changes that take place in the female body as it matures. Margaret Sanger also wrote openly and frankly about feminine hygiene. One admirer described those early articles as providing "scientific information whose intention was to revolutionize women's entire attitude toward sex."[13]

As Margaret Sanger had intended, *The Call* articles stirred up a great deal of controversy. She wanted to destroy complacency and smugness so that a new world of freedom, free love, and free sexual expression for women would emerge.

This type of subject had never before appeared in popular print. Many people were outraged at the frank discussion of public health issues such as syphilis and gonorrhea. Many people were shocked by her open discussion of sexual matters. They applied pressure against the journal's editor to stop publishing such dangerous materials.

Margaret Sanger's articles did not violate the Comstock laws. They did not discuss the subject of contraception. Nevertheless, Margaret Sanger knew that in her urgency to bring basic public health matters to the attention of her patients she was in danger of violating the Comstock Law and the laws of New York State.

She was infuriated by the knowledge that her efforts to help poor women could be seen as illegal. To her the suppression of the articles in *The Call* became a matter of principle. The principle was defense of freedom of speech. Margaret Sanger was moved to take an even more aggressive approach to the whole problem of women's rights in controlling their own bodies.

Sanger's crusade took an important turn when she was ordered to halt publication of her fiery magazine, The Woman Rebel.

The Woman Rebel

Sanger conceived the idea of publishing a periodical exclusively for women. The periodical would become a forum for her crusade. In it, she would discuss the entire matter of reproductive freedom for women whose lives were enslaved by their inability to prevent unwanted pregnancies.

In the course of conversations with her radical friends, Margaret struggled to find a name to describe what she was trying to accomplish. Finally she gave the subject the name by which it has ever since been known—birth control. Thus the birth control movement in the United States was born in 1913.

In 1914 Margaret Sanger launched her new, shockingly radical periodical venture. This was a fiery magazine called *The Woman Rebel*. The first issue of *The Woman Rebel* appeared in March. It adopted a stridently aggressive tone, announcing to the world a new kind of radical journalism that would champion women's rights.

The slogan on the masthead of the first edition, "No Gods, No Masters" revealed Margaret's philosophy. Mrs. Sanger wrote that her intention was "not to preserve a man-made world but to create a human world by the infusion of the feminine element into all its activities."[14]

In June 1914 the words *birth control* appeared in print for the very first time. Sanger also announced that *The Woman Rebel* would soon publish all available information on the subject of contraception.

Margaret Sanger was ordered to desist from publishing such illegal information.

Censorship

Early in her career, Margaret Sanger came up against the censorship imposed by the Comstock laws. She had written several articles for The Call *in 1912 which discussed female hygiene. One Sunday, she sat down to read her latest article and discovered that the hand of the censor had been at work. The following quote is taken from Madeline Gray's book.*

"These articles ran along for three or four weeks until one Sunday morning I turned to the *Call* to see my precious little effort, and, instead, encountered a newspaper box two columns wide in which was printed in black letters,

WHAT EVERY GIRL SHOULD KNOW

N

O

T

H

I

N

G

by order of

THE POST-OFFICE DEPARTMENT

The words gonorrhea and syphilis had occurred in that article and Anthony Comstock, head of the New York Society for the Suppression of Vice, did not like them. By the so-called Comstock Law of 1873, which had been adroitly pushed through a busy Congress on the eve of adjournment, the Post Office had been given authority to decide what might be called lewd, lascivious, indecent, or obscene, and this extraordinary man had been granted the extraordinary power, alone of all citizens of the United States, to open any letter or package or pamphlet or book passing through the mails, and, if he wished, lay his complaint before the Post Office. So powerful had his society become that anything to which he objected in its name was almost automatically barred; he had turned out to be sole censor for ninety million people. During some forty years Comstock had been damming the rising tide of new thought, thereby causing much harm."

The Naming of the Birth Control Movement

In the following excerpt from her Autobiography, *Margaret Sanger describes how the movement which drew its inspiration from her got its name.*

"A new movement was starting, and the baby had to have a name. It did not belong to Socialism nor was it in the labor field, and it had much more to it than just the prevention of conception. As a few companions were sitting with me one evening we debated in turn voluntary parenthood, voluntary motherhood, the new motherhood, constructive generation, and new generation. The terms already in use—Neo-Malthusianism, Family Limitation, and Conscious Generation seemed stuffy and lacked popular appeal.

The word control was good, but I did not like limitation—that was too limiting. I was not advocating a one-child or two-child system as in France, nor did I wholeheartedly agree with the English Neo-Malthusians whose concern was almost entirely with limitation for economic reasons. My idea of control was bigger and freer. I wanted family in it, yet family control did not sound right. We tried population control, race control, and birth rate control. Then someone suggested, 'Drop the rate.' Birth control was the answer; we knew we had it. Our work for that day was done and everybody picked up his hat and went home. The baby was named."

In her biography, Madeline Gray quotes the notice Sanger received from the New York State postal authorities:

> Dear Madame, . . . You are hereby notified that the Solicitor of the Post Office Department has decided that *The Woman Rebel* for March 1914 is unsalable under Sec. 489, Postal Laws and Regulations.[15]

Sanger continued to write articles for the publication, which skirted the edge of violating the Comstock laws. The May, June, and July issues of *The Woman Rebel* were suppressed. The Postal Service refused to send them through the mail. Finally, the full power of the law fell upon her. Margaret Sanger was summoned to appear before the New York City magistrate for violating the Comstock Law. She was informed that, if she admitted that she had violated state and federal laws, she would get off with a light sentence. If, however, she decided to have the case heard, she might be sentenced to a term in jail of up to forty-five years.

Less than two years after beginning her crusade on behalf of women's contraceptive rights, Margaret Sanger had become the center of a national controversy. Yet she still had not published a single piece of information that violated the Comstock laws. Under these circumstances she decided she would not cooperate with the legal system. She would fight it.

She wrote in her diary that it would be very time consuming to prepare a strong argument in her defense before the beginning of her trial. She also knew that if she were imprisoned, the fledgling birth control movement she had begun would wither. So she made a momentous decision that affected the entire course of the birth control movement in America.

Immigrating to Britain

Margaret Sanger decided she had to escape from the United States. She had very little money and no passport. She had no letters of introduction to people influential in the birth control movement in England, a movement that had been active since the 1870s. Nevertheless, she packed a small bag, made arrangements for the care of her three children, and then fled from the United States through Canada under the assumed name of Bertha Watson.

She crossed the submarine-infested Atlantic Ocean in November 1914 in order to get to England. There she intended to prepare her legal defense against the New York State charges. She hoped to accomplish this by studying the subject in a country that no longer made such information illegal.

After three days at sea, Margaret Sanger abandoned all recourse to legal safety. She sent telegrams to friends, telling them to release thousands of copies of a pamphlet called *Family Limitations.*

Family Limitations contained all the information then available on the subject of contraception. In it, she discussed condoms, which were easily available; diaphragms, which were costly; and douches, which if not effective as a birth control technique, aided in avoiding vaginal diseases.

Family Limitations reflected the immature stage of the American birth control movement in 1914. In her youthful enthusiasm Sanger wrote that "any nurse or doctor can teach a woman how to adjust a diaphragm and women can then teach each other."[16] Her views on this critical matter soon would change under the tutelage of the more advanced British and Dutch. Finally, the pamphlet contained diagrams that showed how to use some of the devices that the pamphlet openly discussed and depicted. The pamphlet sold for twenty-five cents. By its publication, Margaret Sanger finally violated the Comstock laws.

Family Limitations became the bible of the birth control movement. Mrs. Sanger's little book was translated into thirteen languages, and eventually ten million copies were circulated throughout the world. In fact, her first stay in England was financed by proceeds of the sale of the pamphlet. Her husband and friends sent her royalties to the fictitious Bertha Watson, in care of American Express, London, England.

3 Acquiring Knowledge to Start a Revolution

When a thing ceases to be a subject of controversy, it ceases to be a subject of interest.

—William Hazlitt

In England Margaret Sanger found a far more active birth control movement than existed in the United States. The battle to be able to openly discuss contraceptive methods already had been fought and won by English radicals in the courts. Curiously, the major court battle was over the right to distribute an American book on contraception.

The 1832 book, *The Fruits of Philosophy*, had been written by Dr. Charles Knowlton of Taunton, Massachusetts, a graduate of Dartmouth College. In it, Knowlton describes various birth control methods.

Knowlton was fined and placed in an East Cambridge, Massachusetts, prison for four months for publishing obscene literature. His book, which was highly technical, was not destroyed, however. Forgotten in the United States, copies of it remained, gathering dust on library shelves.

In England, however, the book was widely but quietly read. Then a Bristol printer, Henry Cook, published an illustrated edition in the 1870s. It was then charged that this new edition was interlaced with sexually explicit pictures which were deemed to be obscene. Since the publication of obscene pictures was against the law, Cook was tried, found guilty of the charges against him, and sentenced to two years imprisonment at hard labor.

The Neo-Malthusian League

An English group called the Neo-Malthusian League decided to challenge the charge. The league supported the ideas of Thomas Malthus, a late-eighteenth-century English economist. Malthus had argued in his 1798 book, *An Essay on the Principle of Population*, that uncontrolled population growth inevitably led to poverty, starvation, and disease. He believed that these terrible social conditions were natural checks on overpopulation, which would then return to a level that could be supported by current economic developments within a country. Only widespread late marriage and sexual abstinence could alter this dismal picture.

The Neo-Malthusian League developed in England in the nineteenth century and was interested in controlling the unrestricted growth of population. They believed that people should marry early but should practice birth control to regu-

The Neo-Malthusian League, inspired by eighteenth-century English economist Thomas Malthus, supported contraception as a means of controlling population growth.

lower court found the two guilty of violating the country's obscenity laws by publishing the book.

Eventually Besant and Bradlaugh won their case. Besant, assisted by Bradlaugh, argued before the Lord Chief Justice Cockburn that it was critical to get contraceptive information to poor people. The case of *Regina vs. Charles Bradlaugh and Annie Besant* was found in favor of the publishers. The right to write about, discuss, and publish information on the subject of birth control was guaranteed under English law as a result of this case.

The legal decision cleared the way for the emergence of many birth control groups. It also allowed for free discussion of human sexuality in a way that was still

Annie Besant (below) and her collaborator Charles Bradlaugh challenged English law by reprinting the illustrated edition of The Fruits of Philosophy *after it had been banned.*

late the size of their families. Members of the league were influential, not only in England, but throughout the world. They decided to make the charge against Henry Cook's publication a test case regarding the free discussion of contraception.

Besant and Bradlaugh

In 1876 two famous English radicals, Annie Besant and Charles Bradlaugh, challenged the English legal system in the matter because they believed that the book was not only decent, but very useful for helping to control unwanted births.

Besant and Bradlaugh established the Freethought Publishing Company for the purpose of reprinting the banned book to test the issue in the English legal system. A

impossible in the United States. Margaret Sanger wanted to make contact with this growing movement.

Sanger's work for *The Call*, *The Woman Rebel*, and *Family Limitations*, had made her well-known among some of the members of the Neo-Malthusian League. After settling herself in a tiny, cold room at 47 Torrington Square near the British Museum, she set out to meet the members of the league.

Sanger and Havelock Ellis

First Margaret Sanger visited the Drysdales, who headed the Neo-Malthusian League. The Drysdale family had been advocating population control for most of the nineteenth century. She also met well-known authors such as H.G. Wells and George Bernard Shaw, who were working for social change. In addition, Sanger met the famous physician and philosopher, Havelock Ellis. They became romantically involved, and she remained on intimate terms with Ellis until his death in 1939.

Ellis's work, *Studies in the Psychology of Sex*, was a revolutionary study of the sexual interaction between males and females. During a forty-year career of research and writing, Ellis attempted to dispel many of the myths associated with the sensitive subject of human sexuality. Ellis explored the uncharted world of emotional reactions to the sexual act and created a revolution in thought about sex. In particular Ellis openly discussed the right of women to experience pleasure in a sexual relationship. This was a very new concept at the beginning of the twentieth century. Sanger found Ellis's thinking and guidance ex-

tremely stimulating in formulating her own ideas about birth control.

Margaret Sanger greatly admired the accomplishments of her new English friends. They, in turn, were impressed by the provocative and courageous stand Sanger had taken against the legal system in the United States. Havelock Ellis once wrote to her saying "I know you are not happy unless you are doing something daring."[17] And H.G. Wells, the noted writer and social radical with whom Sanger also became intimately involved, wrote:

I am inclined to think that there has hitherto been rather too much per-

A romantic relationship developed between Sanger and physician-philosopher Havelock Ellis in 1915. Through his writings, Ellis tried to dispel many myths about human sexuality.

Sanger also had an intimate relationship with writer H.G. Wells. Wells was among those who advised Sanger in her crusade.

America that Sanger's voice be heard. Their advice to Margaret was to concentrate all her efforts on furthering the fight for birth control and to distance herself from other radical causes that would diminish the impact of the birth control campaign. They helped direct her to birth control literature that she could find in the British Museum's collection.

Days at the British Museum

Margaret Sanger spent many long days at the British Museum in 1915. The warmth of the museum contrasted pleasantly with the dismal cold of her small room and encouraged her in her research. From nine in the morning until seven in the evening, she studied the subject of birth control. She plowed through the work of the British theorists Thomas Malthus, Robert Owen, and John Stuart Mill in order to increase her understanding of social economics. She read all she could on the latest techniques of contraception. In particular, she reread much of what Ellis had discussed. Her knowledge of the subject increased dramatically.

In a sense, during this stay in England, Sanger received the formal education her early poverty had denied her. As she studied in the British Museum, her intellectual horizons broadened. She also saw the value of moderating her radicalism to suit the social environment she wished to influence.

Sanger also read extensively about birth control in other countries. She was especially impressed by practices in the Netherlands. There, Dr. Aletta Jacobs and Dr. Johannes Rutgers had opened a chain

sonal emotion spent upon this business, and far too little attention given to its broader aspects. Mrs. Sanger with her extraordinary breadth of outlook and the real scientific quality of her mind, has . . . lifted this question from out of the warm atmosphere of troubled domesticity in which it has hitherto been discussed, to its proper level as a predominantly important human affair.[18]

Ellis, Wells, and the others offered whatever help and advice they could to the young American.

Her new English friends encouraged Sanger in her crusade. They believed that it was critical for the poor women of

Something for the Cause

In England, Margaret Sanger wrote a letter on November 20, 1914, to her sister Mary, in which she describes her activities:

"You will be surprised to hear that I am in England but here I am and all well & happy. I am waiting to visit Edward Carpenter [an advocate of sexual freedom] before I go on to London . . . I am trying to get the interest of the Neo-Malthusian League to help me in my fight against the post-office authorities, and if the war were not taking the attention of the English people I certainly should be able to make an international case of it, & make U.S. puritanical ideas a laughing stock for the world. So if I do lose out in my case & am sent to the federal prison I shall have something to think of & have at least done something for the cause."

While Margaret Sanger was in England, her husband was arrested for distributing copies of Family Limitations. *Sanger wrote to American socialist organizations which had been distributing her pamphlet to explain how she felt about the matter:*

"There is no doubt that my husband's arrest is but a trap of the Government, set to secure my return to the U.S.A., as well as to silence the propaganda of birth control. But we who have hatred and contempt in our hearts for these authorities whose high-handed officialism is running riot in America are not to be deterred from our cause nor trapped in our work because of sentiment; and just as I refuse to go meekly like a lamb to slaughter when I saw that the Court was prejudiced against me, so now do I refuse to be tricked into rushing to the side of my comrade and pal, or to the aid of my three little ones who will be left unprotected by his imprisonment, until I have finished this work which I began to do. The sufferings of one who is loved by me could be no more deeply burned in my soul than the sufferings and anguish of thousands of other women's loved ones left alone in sorrow by death which has been caused by abortion."

The British Museum offered Sanger a chance to broaden her intellectual horizons as well as add to her knowledge of birth control techniques.

of clinics in 1878 in which contraceptive information and techniques were openly provided to patients. These clinics not only had the support of the state, but the Neo-Malthusian League which ran the clinics had been awarded a medal of honor by Wilhelmina, queen of the Netherlands.

A Trip to Holland

Largely due to this clinic system, the maternal death rate in the Netherlands was the lowest in Europe. In fact, it was a third of that experienced in the United States. Furthermore, Amsterdam, the capital of the Netherlands, had the lowest infant death rate of any major world city. The

birth control clinics also appeared to improve the general health of the entire Dutch population. Because of the medicines and information provided by the clinics, death had decreased, houses of prostitution had closed, and the number of illegitimate children had decreased.

Margaret Sanger wanted to see this miracle for herself. She was determined to visit the Netherlands. She had no passport. She spoke no Dutch. But she managed to get to Amsterdam and went to one of Dr. Rutgers's clinics. She noted in her journal that in Holland "contraception was looked on as no more unusual than we in America regard the purchase of a toothbrush."[19]

The clinics of Dr. Rutgers and Dr. Jacobs emphasized maternal health as well as birth control. They believed that women were better mothers if their children

Margaret Sanger went to the Netherlands to visit clinics she had read about in her research. She brought back many ideas that she would use in her own clinic.

were spaced properly. They recommended several years between births. They also believed that healthier mothers bore healthier babies. The proper spacing of children placed fewer strains both on a mother's body and on a family's resources.

Critical to this system of birth control was individualization in the provision of birth control devices. The women who staffed the clinics were trained nurse-midwives. They all had received instruction in fitting women with birth control devices suitable to their ages and body structures. Since Sanger was a nurse, Dr. Rutgers invited her to join a training group to learn these skills.

The type of birth control that Sanger was trained to help women use was a diaphragm which had been developed in Germany in the 1880s by Dr. Wilhelm Mensinga and Dr. Aletta Jacobs. The Mensinga diaphragm eventually was adopted by most western countries. Until the advent of hormonal contraceptives in the 1960s, the Mensinga diaphragm continued to be the most effective method of birth control.

In the Netherlands, clinic staff spent a lot of time making certain that the birth control device fitted properly. Patients were carefully examined by trained technicians, and then each woman was individually and carefully fitted for the appropriate contraceptive device. This was extremely important, since diaphragms were made in fourteen sizes. Clinic staff also instructed patients in the proper care and maintenance of the birth control device.

During her short stay with the Rutgers clinic, Sanger worked to perfect her skills as a fitter of these diaphragms. Dr. Rutgers was so impressed with her ability that he permitted her to fit several patients on her own.

Margaret Sanger's experience in the Netherlands completely changed the nature of the birth control movement in the United States. Until she visited the Rutgers clinic, she had associated the birth control movement with the issue of freedom of speech:

> I had believed in 1914 that the birth control movement would be seen as part of the fight for freedom of speech. It seemed to me then that the information given in pamphlet form and placed in the hands of fathers or mothers would ultimately settle the problem of limiting the family.[20]

The Physician's Role

In the Netherlands Margaret Sanger became convinced that birth control should be discussed and conducted only under a doctor's direction. This position was radically different from that of women's rights advocates in the United States, who continued to see the issue as one of freedom of speech.

Her defense of the role of the physician in birth control made Sanger's battle a difficult one. American physicians refused to associate themselves with radical causes. Yet, in the long run, their ultimate conversion to the birth control movement was critical to its success.

By 1916 Margaret Sanger had come a long way from the radical position she had expressed in *Family Limitations* in 1914. The birth control movement was no longer merely an extension of the right to freedom of speech. It was an extremely serious social concern and had to be treated with respectful professionalism.

Sanger also became convinced that birth control had to be studied scientifically. In this, she felt she could improve on Rutgers's approach. Dr. Rutgers's records were badly maintained. Valuable demographic information was lost, along with the lessons such information could provide to other researchers in the field.

Sanger believed case histories and records had to be kept to advance birth control technology. She foresaw a crusade to make birth control a new science guided by physicians and researchers who were deeply devoted to the welfare of their female patients. This major change in Sanger's approach to birth control indicated that her stay in Europe had been extremely fruitful for her intellectual development. She was ready to resume her battle in America.

She also believed that her increased knowledge of birth control techniques would catapult her to the position of sole spokesperson for birth control in the United States. However, during Sanger's absence in England, several birth control groups had formed in the United States. The most important of these was the National Birth Control League, led by Mary Ware Dennett.

Dennett and her associates made no secret of their desire to keep their distance from Margaret Sanger. They regard-

Mary Ware Dennett headed the National Birth Control League. The league viewed Sanger as a fanatic and tried to steer a more moderate course.

ed Sanger as a fanatic. They remembered her wild language and extravagant claims on behalf of women's rights in 1912 and 1913. The National Birth Control League opposed what it called the "atmosphere of violence" which accompanied many of Margaret Sanger's speeches and public appearances. They believed that moderation would advance the birth control movement faster than Sanger's dramatic approach. This conflict between Sanger and Dennett for dominance in the American birth control movement would continue for many years.

Return to New York

While still in England, however, Sanger believed that she alone was now in a position to fight the battles that would destroy American opposition to the birth control movement. She also understood that she would have to work hard to live down the reputation for radicalism that was associated with her earlier political activism years. She felt invigorated and ready to accept new challenges.

She gathered as many different types of birth control devices as she thought she could smuggle into the United States. Then she booked passage to New York City. Her children eagerly awaited her arrival. The courts also anticipated her return. Sanger, in turn, felt prepared to face the obscenity charges of the court which had been filed against her a year earlier, in 1914.

A great deal had happened since Margaret had escaped to England. Her hasty departure from the United States had not ended the controversy she had begun with

the publication of her pamphlet, *Family Limitations*. Her estranged husband, William Sanger, had been arrested for giving away copies of Margaret's pamphlet. Anthony Comstock personally arrested William Sanger and berated Margaret, author of the pamphlet, as a "heinous criminal."

The judge at William Sanger's trial announced:

> In my opinion, the pamphlet [*Family Limitations*] is not only indecent but immoral. It is not only contrary to the laws of the state but contrary to the laws of God. Any man or woman who would circulate literature of this kind is a menace to the community.[21]

William Sanger was given a thirty-day jail sentence.

The judge hoped that her husband's

During Sanger's absence from the United States, her estranged husband, William, was jailed for distributing copies of her Family Limitations *pamphlet.*

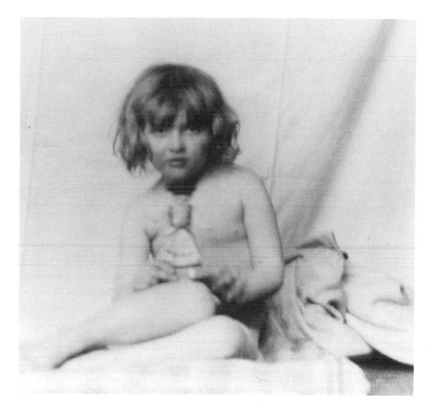

Sanger's only daughter, Peggy, died of pneumonia four months after her mother's return from England. Sanger blamed herself for Peggy's death.

sentencing would cause Sanger to return to the United States to accept responsibility for her violations of federal obscenity laws. When Margaret did not return, William Sanger's imprisonment increased public interest in the birth control movement. When Sanger returned to New York City for her own trial, she was already something of a celebrity.

Before the trial Sanger suffered a personal tragedy. Her eight-year-old daughter Peggy contracted pneumonia soon after Sanger arrived home. Margaret kept constant watch over Peggy during the little girl's illness. But with antibiotics not yet available, Peggy died a mere four months after Margaret's return from Europe. Sanger blamed herself for the rest of her life for her daughter's death.

In her grief over the loss of her daugh-ter, Margaret Sanger dedicated herself even more fanatically to the birth control movement in America. She informed the court that she was prepared to face all the charges filed against her. Sanger hoped the trial would "raise birth control out of the gutter of obscenity and into the light of human understanding."[22] She began to prepare her case, and she also made the dramatic public announcement that she intended to act as her own attorney.

Gaining Public Support

In 1916, however, there was no need for Sanger to fight her legal battles alone. She had begun to gain public sympathy for the campaign she singlemindedly and single-handedly had waged from 1912 to 1915. Peggy's tragic death and the image of the grieving mother that was presented in the national news also lent a new and sympathetic dimension to Sanger's cause.

In addition, Margaret Sanger began to gain the support of New York City's upper class. Influential and wealthy women wanted to meet Sanger. Upon seeing her for the first time, they discovered a slight, pretty, shy woman who dressed conservatively and spoke in a soft, gentle, refined manner. Many people had expected a fire-breathing American version of the impassioned English suffragettes. Instead, only Sanger's words betrayed the intensity of her devotion to her crusade. Many people were pleasantly surprised and decided to work with or for the birth control movement.

Her celebrity status continued to work in Margaret's favor. Shortly before the opening of Sanger's trial in January 1916,

Marie Stopes, an outspoken advocate of birth control in England, appealed to President Woodrow Wilson to halt the criminal trial against Sanger.

Sanger (left) and a friend on their way to Sanger's trial.

Spectators packed the court-room for Sanger's 1916 trial. Among those attending were Sanger's friend, Rose Pastor Stokes (left), and Sanger's sister, Ethel Byrne (right), who pose with Sanger (center) at the courthouse.

President Woodrow Wilson received a special appeal on her behalf. It was written by the famous English birth control advocate Marie Stopes and signed by nine of England's most famous writers. The writers called for "an end to criminal prosecution for circulating material which would be allowed in every civilized country except the United States."[23]

The contents of the letter were widely publicized in the New York City newspapers. Her new, wealthy New York socialite supporters were now even more impressed by Sanger's social views because of her international celebrity. On the eve of the

Sanger trial, two hundred New York society women held a huge pretrial banquet in Margaret's honor at the Brevoort Hotel in New York City.

Fashionable people from the liberal and intellectual worlds attended the event and praised Margaret Sanger's energy and success in battle on behalf of birth control. Columnist Walter Lippmann, Herbert Croly, editor of the *New Republic*, and Viola La Follette, daughter of a famous U.S. senator, were among the attendees.

The next day, January 18, 1916, reporters crowded into the federal building in New York City to hear the opening of

The State of New York vs. Margaret Sanger

When Margaret Sanger returned to the United States, she was determined to have her day in court. The government, however, was less interested in prosecution. As a result of this odd turn of events, the following article appeared in the New York Sun *in February 1915:*

"Mrs. Margaret H. Sanger appeared at the Criminal branch of the United States District Court yesterday to make her weekly demand that she be placed on trial for using the mails in her advocacy of birth control and other subjects which the Government considers improper. Because of the Government's reluctance to be used as an instrument in giving publicity to sex theories at this time, the Sanger case presented the anomaly [irregularity] of a prosecutor loath to prosecute and a defendant anxious to be tried."

The explanation presented by the Court was that

"the case had been laid before the grand jurors as impartially as possible and since they had voted an indictment there was nothing that the District Attorney could not but prosecute. Now, however, as it was realized that the indictment was two years old, and that Mrs. Sanger was not a disorderly person and did not make a practice of publishing such articles, the Government had considered that there was reason for considerable doubt."

the trial against Margaret Sanger on obscenity charges. They vied for seats with many wealthy New York spectators. Newspaper accounts recorded—with astonishment—the number of expensive vehicles that blocked the streets in front of the federal building that day.

Case Dismissed

In the end, Judge Henry D. Clayton bowed to public pressure. First, the court adjourned the trial for a week while several attorneys assigned to the case considered how to proceed. Then, on February 18, 1916, the court entered a *nolle porsequi* (Latin for "to be unwilling to pursue"); that is, the government would not prosecute the case.

Sanger saw the court decision as a great victory for the cause of defending the rights of poor women to prevent unwanted pregnancies. Her case had received national coverage, and the discussion of birth control had come out from behind locked doors.

But nothing had changed legally as a result of the decision not to try her case. It was still illegal to provide contraceptives to women. Moreover, the churches in America still opposed birth control. The Comstock regulations still were the law of the land, and Theodore Roosevelt continued to rail about the nationalistic responsibility of women to have large families.

After the case against Margaret Sanger was dismissed, the *New York Globe* best captured the essence of the situation when it wrote in an editorial,

> The right of American citizens to discuss sociological questions according to their convictions is just where it was before—subject to the mutton-headed restrictions of some post office clerk and the complaisant persecution of a Federal district attorney.[24]

This dismal mood, however, was not entirely justifiable. Margaret Sanger was not in jail. She had forced the government to retreat from its extreme position. But if birth control were to become the right of every woman in the United States, Margaret Sanger would have to take her fight to the entire country. As a free person she was in a position to launch that campaign. She knew she would have to maintain the momentum and enthusiasm that her trial had aroused.

4 The Fight for Birth Control Clinics

The most important force in the remaking of the world is a free motherhood.

—Margaret Sanger

In the days before the 1916 trial, Margaret Sanger received thousands of letters from people all over the country. Many were letters of encouragement. Many others were invitations to speak. Although she was a shy person who had never enjoyed addressing large groups of people, she knew she would have to overcome her fears if she were to bring birth control information to the poor women of America. She drafted a speech that contained the essential elements of her message to the American people. She practiced the speech so that she would not become tongue-tied, even if she were physically attacked or her audience became hostile. Then she set out to deliver her message across America.

At 119 stops in cities and towns across the United States, Margaret Sanger urged people to "raise the question of birth control out of the gutter of obscenity, where my opponents have put it, and get it into the light of intelligence and human understanding." She told the crowds who came to hear her that "the first right of every child is to be desired, to be planned with a natural intensity of love that gives it its title to being."[25]

Repeatedly, passionately, Margaret Sanger announced her belief that

> Birth control is the key note of a new social awakening, an awakening of the parent towards a responsibility for its offspring, an awakening of the individual toward the consequences of his act. It is not only a welfare and economic expedient. It is a great social principle.[26]

She movingly described the plight of the poor women who lived in the tenements of New York City, trying desperately to prevent bearing more children.

> To see those pale-faced mothers . . . their faces pinched and wan from overwork and worry, crowding forward, eager to face the torture of abortion rather than condemn their unborn children to poverty—to see this was enough to make one's blood boil with rage at the hypocritical silence of the medical profession who cater to the whims of the rich but ignore the tragedy of the poor.[27]

These were powerful images. Sanger was describing access to birth control measures as a class issue—the haves against the have-nots. Clearly, she believed that poor women were denied access to birth

Sanger was haunted by the wan faces of women and their families in tenements and their willingness to obtain abortions in unsanitary and dangerous conditions.

control, while rich women could easily receive it in the offices of their private physicians.

Sanger's Nonthreatening Appearance

A more aggressive-appearing woman might have offended her audiences by bringing up these issues. But Margaret Sanger's femininity disarmed them. Her simple, carefully chosen clothes were modest and unassuming. And she always spoke softly. Her appearance helped people to accept her message, and increasing numbers of people were profoundly affected by her. The middle- and upper-class people who paid to hear Sanger speak were moved by her forceful appeal to women and about women's issues in general.

As a result of her first national speaking tour in 1916, Margaret Sanger became

a major voice for the American women's movement. In addition to speaking about birth control, she encouraged women to step out of their traditional, procreative roles. Maternity should be a choice, she told them, not an obligation. Women should be free to explore other avenues of fulfillment besides motherhood.

In part because of her nonthreatening approach, many birth control leagues sprang up in the cities where Sanger had spoken. The members of these leagues enlisted still more people. They in turn became part of the movement to try to overturn the antiquated Comstock Law and other barriers to full political and economic equality for women.

The Church's Opposition

Still, the three-and-a-half-month speaking tour was not a total success. In fact it had an ominous, dark side. In St. Louis, for example, Sanger encountered the open animosity of the hierarchy of the Roman Catholic church. The church used its influence to prevent Sanger from speaking at the Victoria Theater, even though the theater had been rented long in advance for her to address the community. On the evening of her intended speech, it was locked. Its owner could not be found.

The church wanted to stop her from speaking because it opposed birth control on scriptural grounds. According to Roman Catholic doctrine, the sole purpose of sexual relations between husband and wife is to create new life. The church saw the growing birth control movement and Margaret Sanger as threats to this basic tenet.

The episode in St. Louis was the first round in what would become a long, drawn out battle between Sanger and the Roman Catholic church. Throughout Sanger's career, the Catholic church would use its enormous financial and political resources to try to crush the campaign for reproductive freedom in the United States.

Establishing a Clinic

The conflict began in earnest when Margaret Sanger returned to New York City. Although the trip across the country had been exhausting, Sanger was exhilarated by her enormous success and decided to do more than give speeches. She decided to establish a clinic where she could provide the services she had discussed during her speaking tour. She hoped that a successful clinic in New York City would be only the first of many she would establish all over the country.

This was an extremely dangerous undertaking. The Comstock Law prohibited the distribution of birth control information. Physicians still regarded her as an irresponsible and dangerous crank. Protestant churches, as well as the Roman Catholic church, opposed her. In New York City these enemies were especially dangerous because Roman Catholic church politics played a large role in police matters. The church was very wealthy, made large contributions to police organizations, and expected favors in return. Would the civil authorities permit Sanger to run a clinic?

Sanger was willing to find out. She intended to oppose them all and challenge laws she thought were absurd and antiquated. But she needed some organizational support to help finance her undertaking. She refused to join the National Birth Control League headed by Mrs. Dennett. Instead, she formed an organization called the New York Birth Control League to serve as her base of operations and which she would control personally.

She also began publishing a periodical, which she called the *Birth Control Review* in which she could publicize her activities. In it she announced that "if a woman must break the law to establish her right to voluntary motherhood, then that law must be broken."[28]

Margaret Sanger, her sister Ethel Byrne (who was also a nurse), and a close friend and associate named Fania Mindell set out to challenge the law. They were determined to open a clinic where poor women could obtain birth control information. Margaret Sanger intended to use the knowledge she had gained while working with Dr. Rutgers in the Netherlands to

A Physician's Advice

As Margaret Sanger prepared to open her clinic in Brooklyn she received a letter from Dr. William J. Robinson who was sympathetic to her cause but did not feel comfortable assisting her. In the letter, excerpted here from Madeline Gray's book, Robinson does, however, give her advice:

"The American Medical Association cannot and will not in any way interfere with you. It is outside of its domain. The only Society that could have something to say would be the New York County Medical Society, but I am quite certain that you need fear nothing at their hands, because their province is only to interfere with illegal practitioners, with people who treat disease. As you will not deal with treatment, only with hygienic advice, they can have nothing to say to you. Neither can the Federal authorities. The only people you have to be afraid of are the States authorities, or the Vice Society.

The first and most important thing is to have every woman who applies for advice sign a slip that says she is a married woman and that she wants the information for her personal use, as for either hygienic, hereditary, or economic reasons she feels herself unable to have any more children. Of course you cannot demand that the women bring their marriage certificates, but the fact alone that they sign such a statement would absolve you from any blame and from any possible accusations of fostering "immorality." If you should publicly declare yourself willing to give that information to unmarried women you would have the law down on you at once.

If you do as I say, and if you don't charge the people anything for advice, which I know you won't, they would have great difficulty in doing anything to you, and this Birth Control Clinic might become the germ of thousands of similar clinics."

help New York City's neediest families.

Margaret, Ethel, and Fania walked the streets of Brooklyn, looking for the ideal spot to open their clinic. After some searching, they found a place on Amboy Street near the corner of Pitkin Avenue, in the Brownsville section of Brooklyn.

The landlord, Joseph Rabinowitz, was friendly and willing to accept fifty dollars a month for the rental of a small but suitable apartment. The location was ideal. The population of the neighborhood was fairly evenly divided among Jewish, Catholic, and Protestant families. Most im-

A devoted follower distributes Sanger's periodical, Birth Control Review.

seven in the morning on that first day, 140 people lined up along Amboy Street to gain admission to the clinic.

They came singly, some with other women, a few with their husbands. Many brought along several small children. They paid ten cents a visit to find out how they could avoid having unwanted children. Many of these women hoped to gain useful information that would stop their frequent visits to the neighborhood abortionist and the danger to their health and lives that those repeated visits posed. Many years later, Margaret Sanger wrote, "I believed then and do so today, that the opening of those doors to the mothers of Brownsville was an event of social significance in the lives of American womanhood."[29]

The three women maintained a warm but professional atmosphere in the clinic. Margaret, Ethel, and Fania met with the women individually. If the woman was unmarried, she would not be accepted as a clinic client. Only married women were accepted, because Sanger did not want to be accused of encouraging illicit sex among unmarried people.

Once a prospective client was deemed eligible, Fania Mindell obtained demographic information about her: she recorded the client's name, address, age, ages of living children, number of miscarriages she had experienced, number of abortions she had undergone, and her husband's job and current salary. All this information was kept in neatly arranged files. Sanger wanted the clinic's cumulative experience to provide well-documented social and economic information about the impact of birth control on the community.

Once the forms were completed, one

portantly, the families were headed by poor immigrants who had many children and no knowledge of birth control.

Margaret, Ethel, and Fania washed and painted the walls and repaired windows. They bought secondhand furniture for the clinic. Then they advertised its opening in the local newspaper. The advertisement was printed in Yiddish, English, and Italian. They waited anxiously. Would anyone come?

On October 16, 1917, they opened the doors of the first birth control clinic in the United States. Once the doors were open, their concerns were laid to rest. Starting at

Advertising the Clinic

The fliers for the Sanger clinic, taken from David M. Kennedy's book, were written in English, Yiddish, and Italian and read:

MOTHERS

Can you afford to have a large family?

Do you want any more children?

If not, why do you have them?

DO NOT KILL. DO NOT TAKE LIFE, BUT PREVENT.

Safe, harmless information can be obtained of

Nurses at
46 Amboy Street
Near Pitkin Ave.—Brooklyn

Tell your friends and neighbors. All mothers welcome. A registration fee of 10 cents entitles any mother to this information.

MOTHERS!

Can you afford to have a large family?
Do you want any more children?
If not, why do you have them?
DO NOT KILL, DO NOT TAKE LIFE, BUT PREVENT
Safe, Harmless Information can be obtained of trained
Nurses at
46 AMBOY STREET
NEAR PITKIN AVE. — BROOKLYN.
Tell Your Friends and Neighbors.   All Mothers Welcome
A registration fee of 10 cents entitles any mother to this information.

מומערס!

זיים איהר פערמעגליך צו האבען א גרויסע פאמיליע?
ווילט איהר האבען נאך קינדער?
אויב ניט, ווארום האט איהר זיי?
מערדערט ניט, נעהמט ניט קיין לעבען, נור פערהים זיך.
זיכערע, אונשעדליכע אינפארמאציע קענט איהר בעקומען פון טראאינענע נוירסעס אין
46 אמבאי סטרים ניער פיטקין עוועניו **ברוקלין**
זאגט דאס בעקאנטע צו אייערע פריינד און שכנות.
 יעדער מוטער איז ווילקאמען.
פאר 10 סענט אינטער-ביעגעלד קענען איהר בעקומען צו דיעזע אינפארמעישאן.

MADRI!

Potete permettervi il lusso d'avere altri bambini?
Ne volete ancora?
Se non ne volete piu', perche' continuate a metterli al mondo?
NON UCCIDETE MA PREVENITE!
Informazioni sicuro od innocue saranno fornito da infermiere autorizzate a
46 AMBOY STREET   Near Pitkin Ave. Brooklyn
a cominciare dal 12 Ottobre. Avvertito le vostre amiche e vicine.
Tutte le madri sono ben accette. La tassa d'iscrizione di 10 cents da diritto a qualunque madre di ricevere consigli ed informazioni gratis.
Margaret H. Sanger

One of the many fliers Sanger used to announce birth control assistance in Brooklyn's Brownsville section.

of the two nurses (Margaret or Ethel) met with the client to provide her with birth control information. They used plastic models and pictures to show how conception was prevented. They estimated the size of the birth control device a woman would need. The estimate was based on the number of her past births, miscarriages, and abortions.

The woman then was sent to a druggist to buy a birth control device. They hoped that the woman would be able to

Women anxiously wait outside Sanger's Amboy Street clinic. Some came alone while others brought their children and their husbands with them.

find a cooperative druggist who would fill the written orders. The three women would not fit and sell the devices themselves because the Amboy Street clinic was not under the supervision of a physician. So Margaret and Ethel carefully avoided performing any procedure that was beyond the scope of their training.

Arrested

The clinic was an enormous success. But it had been open only nine days when the police struck. They burst in, confiscated confidential files, and took the names and addresses of the terrified women waiting to be seen. The police behaved as if they had just raided a brothel. Then they arrested the proprietors.

Margaret and Ethel were charged with violating New York State law by operating what the magistrate called a "public nuisance." It was certainly true that the actions of the sisters were in violation of the New York State Penal Code, Section 1142. This section made it a misdemeanor for anyone to "sell, lend, or give away or to advertise, loan or distribute any recipe, drug or medicine for the prevention of conception."[30] Fania was charged with selling indecent books because she sold to anyone who wished them the current editions of *The Birth Control Review.*

Ethel's trial came first. The court found her guilty of having violated the New York State Penal Code. On January 22, 1917, Ethyl Bryne was sentenced to thirty days in prison, to be served in the workhouse on Blackwell's Island on the East River. As she was led away, Ethel vowed that she would take neither bread nor water until she was released from prison. The New York City authorities now had on their hands a woman who was willing to become a martyr to defend a woman's right to obtain contraceptive information.

A Hunger Strike

Ethel became very ill 103 hours into her hunger strike. The prison authorities were afraid she would die, so they decided to force-feed her. This was to be the first time in American history that a woman held in prison would be force-fed. Such treatment was considered to be a form of torture. Its use showed the authorities' fear that Ethel Byrne might become a martyr and attract a protest movement willing to support her.

The prison guards wrapped Byrne in

Ethel Byrne (right) and Sanger at Sanger's 1916 trial. A year after this picture was taken, Byrne also faced trial. She was convicted and sentenced to thirty days in prison.

(From left to right) Fania Mindell, Harold Hersey, and Marion Bloom on their way to the 1917 trial.

blankets to prevent her from struggling. Then they roughly shoved a feeding tube down her throat and poured in a mixture of milk, eggs, and a stimulant. Ethel Byrne suffered terribly from the experience. Her throat was badly bruised and she frequently spit blood. Many friends and supporters feared she was close to death.

Margaret was frantic. She rushed to Albany and finally convinced the governor of New York state, Charles S. Whitman, to release her sister. In exchange, Margaret promised on behalf of Ethel that her sister would hereafter abide by state laws about providing contraceptive information.

Margaret raced to the Blackwell Island workhouse, where she found her sister semiconscious. Margaret and some friends carried Ethel home. It was several weeks before Ethel's survival was assured, and a year before she recovered completely.

Reaction to Ethel's Imprisonment

The press was divided in its response to Ethel Byrne's ordeal. The *St. Paul Dispatch* observed that "the humiliation and righteous indignation felt by every American who has a drop of red blood in his body after reading about Mrs. Byrne cannot be expressed in words."[31]

Other newspapers, however, were unmoved. The *Milwaukee Free Press* wrote: "Is there no limit to the mischief which idle women, inspired and abetted by masculine cranks, can work to modern society?"[32]

Admirers, however, were greatly affected by Ethel Byrne's ordeal. Sanger's secretary, Anna Lifschiz, compared it to a religious crusade. Sanger said of her sister's ordeal that "no single act of self-sacrifice in the history of the birth control movement had done more to awaken the conscience of the country."[33]

In the meantime Margaret was sentenced to thirty days in prison for having violated the Comstock Law. A copy of her pamphlet, *Family Limitations*, had been introduced into court. It contained a picture of a cervical cap that could be used to prevent conception. She later wrote that a federal agent

> read aloud my advice to women to use it as a means of preventing conception. Not even the most friendly judge could get away from the fact that I had intended a far broader definition than any permitted by the existing law.[34]

Sanger served her term in the Queens County Penitentiary in Long Island City. She did not go on a hunger strike. She was afraid that her tuberculosis would recur. But she refused to be fingerprinted and refused to work. Instead she used her time in prison to teach her fellow inmates about birth control. When Margaret was released on March 6, 1917, her supporters greeted her at the prison gates and celebrated her return to them.

More Flock to the Cause

The ordeal of the Higgins sisters created a sensation in America because of the press coverage they received. Millions of people became aware of the battle being waged by a small group of women in New York to put an end to the harsh consequences of the Comstock Law. Many new recruits

Juliet Barrett Rublee joined other well-to-do women to form the Committee of One Hundred.

flocked to their cause. They were impressed by Ethel's heroism and Margaret's devotion and determination. The New York Birth Control League grew as many well-to-do women in New York City offered their time and financial assistance.

For example, Juliet Barrett Rublee, the wife of a rich international lawyer, Mrs. Pinchot, wife of the governor of Pennsylvania, and others formed a Committee of One Hundred. The committee consisted of one hundred socially prominent people who wanted to defend Margaret and Ethel. During the imprisonment of the Higgins sisters, the committee members wrote letters of protest to Washington. They hired Carnegie Hall in New

J.J. Goldstein, posing years later for a photograph, appealed Sanger's conviction free of charge. Sanger lost her appeal but the judge's decision opened the way for more birth control clinics.

York City to stage a protest event on their behalf. Their support continued long after Ethel and Margaret were freed from prison.

Margaret Sanger also received assistance from some members of the legal profession. For example, there was J.J. Goldstein, a young New York attorney who would later gain great prominence as counsel for the American Civil Liberties Union. Goldstein strongly supported the birth control movement and formed a close attachment to Margaret that lasted for many years. He also agreed to appeal the Sanger case, free of charge.

Sanger well knew that in England the reversal of a lower-court decision in the Besant-Bradlaugh case had freed the discussion of birth control from legal constraints. With Goldstein's help, she intended to repeat this victory throughout the United States.

The Crane Decision

Eventually the case was heard by the Supreme Court of New York state. Despite a well-developed argument presented by Goldstein, the presiding judge, Frederick E. Crane of the Appellate Division, upheld the lower court's decision. He found that Sanger had violated Section 1142 of the New York State Penal Code. Her thirty-day sentence was upheld. But Crane also left room for hope. The original charges against Sanger were held to be legal, not because of the information she gave patients, but because she was not a physician. In other words, Judge Crane held that under Section 1145 of the code, a *physician* could give contraceptive advice for the prevention of disease.

Judge Crane defined the word *disease* very broadly. To him it meant "any change in the state of the body which caused or threatened pain and sickness."[35] This new interpretation of the law meant that a physician could determine whether or not a married woman should use contraceptive methods. The Crane decision of 1918 was a major landmark in the fight for reproductive freedom in the United States. The decision provided Sanger with a judicial interpretation that would enable her to carry on the fight to establish birth control clinics all over the country.

The Crane decision made possible the development of clinics such as Sanger had seen in the Netherlands. If Sanger could match the court's requirement that birth

Repudiating Past Tactics

On the eve of her trial in January 1916, Margaret Sanger made a speech at the Brevoort Hotel in New York City. In this speech, taken from Madeline Gray's biography, Sanger apologized for some of the things she had said in the past.

"I realize keenly that many of those who understand and would support the birth-control propaganda if it were carried out in a safe and sane manner cannot sympathize with the methods I have followed in my attempt to arouse working women to the fact that bringing a child into the world is the greatest responsibility. . . .

I know that all of you are better able to cope with the subject than I am. I know that physicians and scientists have a fund of information greater than I have on the subject of family limitation. . . .

WE KNOW TOO, that when the practice of abortion was put under the ban by the church, an alternative evil—the foundling asylum, with its horrifying history—sprang up. THERE IS NO NEED to go into the terrible facts concerning the recklessness, the misery, the filth, with which children have been and still are being brought into the world. . . .

I found it was up to me to shout out the warning! THE TONE OF THE VOICE may have been indelicate and unladylike, and was not at all the tone that many of us would rather hear.

BUT THIS VERY GATHERING—this honor you have thrust upon me—is ample proof that intelligence and constructive thought has been aroused. SOME OF US may only be fit to dramatize a situation—to focus attention upon obsolete laws. . . . Then, others, more experienced in constructive organization can gather together all this sympathy and interest which has been aroused, and direct it. . . .

MY REQUEST TO YOU TONIGHT is that all you social workers—so much better fitted to carry on this work than I—that you consider and organize this interest. THIS IS THE MOST IMPORTANT STEP, AND IN THIS WAY CAN I BE VINDICATED!! LET US PUT THE UNITED STATES OF AMERICA UPON THE MAP OF THE CIVILIZED WORLD!!"

*Sanger leaves the courthouse
after her arraignment on
October 16.*

control devices be prescribed and fitted only under the supervision of a physician, she might be successful.

Now, according to the Crane decision, doctors in New York state no longer had to fear losing their licenses for providing contraceptive information to married women for health reasons. They also were not in danger of lengthy prison sentences for practicing their professions. Now, all Margaret Sanger had to do was find a doc-

tor willing to assist her in the struggle for women's reproductive rights. Then she could open another clinic and test the willingness of the authorities to uphold the Crane decision.

Margaret Sanger clearly now considered herself to be the leader of the American birth control movement. She hoped that her notoriety would be sufficient to attract a courageous physician to step forward to help her.

Chapter

5 Refining the Birth Control Movement

To throttle free speech is to give it a megaphone.

—The New York Globe, 1916

Before Margaret Sanger actually began her new clinic, she decided to hold a birth control conference in New York City. She wanted to familiarize as many people as possible with the progress and success of the movement since 1912. She also wanted to gain national support for her next challenge.

She was assisted in organizing the con-

ference by many upper-class women in New York City who had adopted the birth control movement as their own cause. Many liked the excitement of belonging to an active movement. They had free time and, more importantly, a good deal of money to contribute. Margaret Sanger enjoyed the role of leading a movement whose adherents came from backgrounds far more prosperous than her own.

On the eve of the conference, November 11, 1922, a group of Sanger's followers

The movement to establish birth control clinics nation-wide gained momentum in the 1920s, with Sanger in the lead.

and supporters met to form a new organization: the American Birth Control League. Its board consisted largely of the people who had helped to organize the conference. The league's objectives were

> to build up public opinion so that women should be able to demand instruction from doctors, to assemble the findings of scientists, to remove hampering Federal statutes, to send out field workers into those states where laws did not prevent clinics, to co-operate with similar bodies in studying population problems, food supplies, world peace.[36]

The inauguration of this new organization provided additional support for the conference. Margaret Sanger was selected as its first president.

The conference consisted of seminars and lectures and open and closed meetings dealing with various aspects of the birth control movement. Prominent Europeans who attended the conference reported favorably on its progress in their national newspapers.

In fact, all went well until the conference's culminating event. Margaret Sanger and Dr. Royal S. Copeland, the health commissioner of New York City, were scheduled to participate in a discussion at the town hall entitled "Birth Control: Is It Moral?"

A Second Arrest

When Sanger and her party arrived at the town hall, they discovered that the doors of the auditorium were locked and guarded by New York City police. An angry mob of ticket-holding people massed in front of the entrance to the building. Another angry group found themselves locked inside the hall. Margaret Sanger managed to sneak past the guards and, despite the uproar in the hall, began to address the audience.

The crowd suddenly quieted to listen to Margaret Sanger's soft voice. The police in the hall then arrested Margaret before she could complete even one sentence. They also arrested every subsequent speaker who tried to deliver an address. Watching the police proceedings from the wings of the hall was Monsignor Joseph P. Dineen, secretary to Patrick J. Hayes, the Roman Catholic archbishop of New York City.

Many people besides Margaret Sanger were arrested that evening. They were led through the streets to the local police station and were followed by a shrieking crowd of supporters. One newsman said that the procession to the police station "was one of the wildest parades that New York ever had seen."[37] An investigation of the events subsequently revealed that the Roman Catholic hierarchy of New York City had directed the police to break up the meeting and prevent an open, public discussion of birth control.

Sanger used the unsavory incident to cast herself and her movement in the role of defenders of the Constitution of the United States. She charged that her rights to free speech and freedom of assembly had been violated. It was her view that the constitutional guarantee of the separation of church and state had been violated by the police in New York City, who had openly assisted members of the clergy in shutting down her meeting.

In fact, the charges against her were

The Words the Church Wanted to Suppress

The Catholic church stopped Margaret Sanger from giving her speech at Town Hall. So on November 19, 1922, she rented a larger hall, the Park Theater at Columbus Circle, and gave the speech the church had tried to silence. The speech is excerpted from Madeline Gray's biography.

"Responsible sex-action requires forethought, and irresponsible action is immoral. Every civilization involves an increasing forethought for others, even for those unborn. The reckless abandonment of the moment and the careless regard for the consequences, is not morality. . . . It is not only inevitable, but it is also right that we learn to control the size of our family, for by this control and adjustment we can raise the standards of the human race. . . . Nature's way of reducing her numbers is controlled by disease and famine. Primitive man achieved the same results by infanticide, abandonment of children or abortion. . . . Contraception is a more civilized method, for it involves not only a greater forethought for others, but finally a higher sanction for the value of life itself.

The law requires a married woman to give of herself to her husband or forego his support. This makes self-control by women impractical, if not impossible. . . . And the argument that the use of the marriage relationship is only for the purpose of procreation would conceivably have to limit unions to only a few times in the course of a marriage. . . . This last is perfectly absurd because it places man on the same level as animals. . . . There is another side, another use of the marriage relationship. I contend that it is just as sacred and beautiful for two people to express their love when they have no intention of being parents, and that they can go into that relationship with the same beauty and the same holiness with which they go into music or to prayer. I believe that it is the right understanding of our sexual power and of its creative energy that gives us spiritual illumination. I say that there is more than one use to make of it, and that it is the higher use, the development of our soul and soul growth."

dismissed, because they were baseless. Foolishly, the police had silenced her before she had a chance to speak in violation of the Comstock laws.

Arrest Leads to Support

In many ways the events of 1922 marked a turning point in Sanger's career. Many newspapers had previously opposed the birth control movement; editors were reluctant to speak out on behalf of so radical a social cause. But now Sanger's opponent, the Roman Catholic church, had gone too far in trying to silence the birth control advocates.

The *New York Tribune* said:

The police broke up the meeting without waiting for any expression of opin-

ion which would warrant repression. It was arbitrary and Prussian to the last degree. If the police deny even the right of assemblage to one group of citizens, what is to stop them from denying it to another group against which they or their advisors have a personal prejudice?[38]

The *New York Post* added: "If people cannot come together in a perfectly orderly and open way to debate whether or not a matter is moral, then our boasted freedom of speech is a mockery."[39]

Everybody agreed that the church had gone too far in trying to suppress an open discussion. Many important New York citizens expressed their concern by sending a joint letter to Mayor George Hyland. In it they denounced the police for supporting Archbishop Hayes's efforts to control free speech in the city of New York. Such inter-

---

A Witty Retort

The following excerpt from Sanger's Autobiography *demonstrates the kind of exchange that occurred between her and the Catholic church. This encounter took place in 1918 during a speaking engagement in Connecticut.*

"A young priest stood forth as our chief opponent, basing his objections on the laws of nature, which he claimed were contravened by birth control. Fortunately the committee had a sense of humor. In my ten-minute rebuttal I was able to answer the 'against nature' as Francis Place [an English social reformer] had done a hundred years earlier. I turned the priest's own words on himself by asking why he should counteract nature's decree of impaired vision by wearing eye glasses, and why, above all, was he celibate, thus outraging nature's primary demand on the human species—to propagate its kind. The laughter practically ended the 'unnatural' thesis for a time."

The waiting room at the Clinical Research Bureau. The clinic opened its doors to the public in January 1923.

ference increased sympathy throughout the United States for the birth control movement.

Archbishop Hayes was unrepentant. He continued his attack against Margaret Sanger and her followers. Hayes delivered an official letter in 1922 in which he made clear that the battle was not over: "To take life after its inception is a horrible crime," he told his flock, "but to prevent human life that the Creator is about to bring into being, is satanic."[40]

A New Clinic

Still, Margaret Sanger judged that she had by now gained enough public sympathy to attempt opening a new clinic. The thousands of letters she received begging for birth control information convinced her that the need for such a clinic was enormous.

She knew there would be opposition to the new clinic, so she took steps to

Opposition of the Roman Catholic Church

The Roman Catholic church was opposed to the birth control movement on theological grounds. In this excerpt from Sanger's Autobiography, *she describes some of the obstacles placed in her path by the church.*

"I remember almost innumerable instances of crude and usually unsuccessful attempts to silence me in those days—hotels boycotted by such organizations as the Knights of Columbus because the managers had purveyed luncheons to birth control advocates, halls, contracted and paid for, barred at the last minute on account of Catholic Church pressure brought to bear on owners; permits to hold meetings withdrawn by mayors or other officials in cities having powerful Roman Catholic constituencies.

Boston still remains the one city whose Mayor, Curley, threatened the loss of license to any manager of a hall or theater who allowed me to speak. The Civil Liberties Union still has this threat in its file. I have offered myself on the scaffold of Free Speech any time the citizens of Boston request me to come to make the fight."

avoid the most obvious pitfalls. She kept the new clinic completely independent from the American Birth Control League in order to protect both organizations. She gave it a scientific-sounding name, the Clinical Research Bureau. Many years later it would be known as the Margaret Sanger Research Bureau.

The first of the new clinics was located, not in Brooklyn, but at a fashionable Manhattan address—104 Fifth Avenue. Sanger insisted that, while the politics of the institution remained under her own control, the clinic itself would have a physician as its director.

It took some time to find a doctor who was willing to take the job. Sanger told each applicant that he or she would have

"to stand up . . . under this [Crane] legal opinion" but such an individual would "give tremendous impetus and encouragement to thousands of other doctors throughout the country to do likewise."[41]

Dr. Dorothy Bocker of the Georgia Public Health Service finally agreed to work for Margaret Sanger. Dr. Bocker even accepted the comparatively low salary of five thousand dollars a year. Bocker did not have the kind of experience Sanger would have preferred, but in 1923 Sanger was glad that any physician had accepted the dangerous position.

The Clinical Research Bureau opened its doors to the public in January 1923. From the start the clinic operated on a legal and scientific basis. Only married women could use the services of the clinic. Diaphragms and other birth control techniques were suggested only after complete examination of patients. Clinic staff kept cards that contained full demographic and personal information on each client.

Mrs. Sanger and her staff wanted to collect such information to start a data base. Among other clinical issues, they wanted to study mother-and-child health concerns and the effectiveness of different types of diaphragms. They also wanted to study whether the clinic had an affect on the spacing of its clients' children. The clinic could then share its information with other clinics regarding the most useful birth control techniques. They could begin to document short- and long-range outcomes of birth control on a large population.

Margaret Sanger hoped that other clinics would soon be established and copy these rigorous methodologies. The birth control movement would thereby become a scientific as well as a humanitarian and women's rights movement.

The clinic was an enormous success and fulfilled Sanger's greatest expectations. It gradually became a major resource for gynecological information in the United States. Students from medical schools came to observe clinic proceedings. Data gathered at the clinic formed the basis for publicly delivered research papers. Other cities began to copy the New York clinic's example.

The country's second birth control clinic opened its doors in Chicago in 1924. The Roman Catholic hierarchy tried to use the legal system to prevent this from happening. But Judge Harry Fisher ruled that "courts cannot be called upon to officially interpret the bible or to lend

or withhold their processes to enforce biblical injunctions."[42]

By 1930 there were fifty-five birth control clinics throughout the United States in twelve different states. Sanger's dream was becoming a reality faster than anyone could have anticipated.

The Clinical Research Bureau itself began to expand the number of services it offered. In 1924 the clinic began offering evening hours. It also hired a new medical director, Dr. Hannah Stone, a remarkably skilled physician with extensive experience and special training in women's medicine.

Dr. Stone's support for the birth control movement was heightened by the behavior of her superiors when she was employed in a New York City hospital. When

As medical director, Dr. Hannah Stone helped guide the clinic's efforts in birth control and health education.

the medical director there told her that "no doctor at this hospital can be associated with birth control," she quit.[43]

Dr. Stone immediately joined the staff of the Clinical Research Bureau. The partnership between Margaret Sanger and Hannah Stone lasted for eighteen years. Sanger raised money, gained more public support, and waged her crusade on behalf of the birth control movement. Dr. Stone's driving efforts brought enormous and outstanding scientific progress not only in the field of birth control, but also in health education for women.

By 1925 the Clinical Research Bureau had outgrown its Fifth Avenue site. The clinic moved to a building located on Fifteenth Street. By then it was providing services to 1,655 patients a year. In 1929, 9,737 women were able to obtain birth control information from the clinic.

Careful Records Provide Research Tools

The clinic's records, carefully compiled by the staff, provided a wealth of information for population studies. For example, in 1925, over 70 percent of the women who came to the clinic had husbands who earned less than fifty dollars a week; the average was thirty-six dollars a week. Of the 1,655 patients who came to the clinic that year, 1,434—87 percent—reported having performed self-induced abortions in the past. Clinic records indicated that 38 percent of the patients were Protestant, 32 percent Jewish, and 26 percent Catholic.

The clinic collected information sufficient to keep a research team busy for years. Despite its clinical success and its usefulness as a research center, the Clinical Research Bureau, and the entire birth control movement, were kept at arm's length by the American Medical Association. Sanger and her second husband, J. Noah Slee, whom she married in 1922, tried to break down some of this hostility.

Mr. Slee was a successful businessman from South Africa with a good deal of money to spend on his wife's lifework. Sanger and Slee thought that a better understanding of the movement might help to eliminate some of the American Medical Association's misgivings and perhaps even gain its support.

Dr. Cooper

In 1925 they hired a new physician, a gynecologist named Dr. James F. Cooper, to assist in their efforts to educate the medical profession. Dr. Cooper's credentials were impressive. He had been a medical missionary in China and had had a lucrative private gynecological practice in New York. He gave up this practice to advance the birth control movement.

Sanger wanted Dr. Cooper to travel around the country to speak to his colleagues about birth control. By the end of 1926 he had discussed birth control at the medical associations of every state in the country. He emphasized the importance not only of contraception, but also of spacing children's births in a family. He told his colleagues that the health and well-being of the entire country depended on this kind of population control. In two years Cooper made nearly seven hundred speeches.

Sanger walks with her second husband, J. Noah Slee, in 1927. Slee contributed a great deal of money toward furthering Sanger's work.

As a result of his efforts, many individual physicians began to appreciate the need for the type of medical information provided by Sanger's clinic. Some even came to believe that the medical profession was lagging behind the needs of the community in the area of birth control.

Dr. Robert L. Dickinson, a senior gynecologist at Brooklyn Hospital and a professor of gynecology and medicine at Long Island Medical College, was one of the first to come over to the movement. Since he was recognized as the most prestigious of American gynecologists, his views carried a good deal of weight within the medical profession.

Dr. Dickinson contacted Sanger. Although the two agreed on the need for further education, they clashed over how to pursue their mutual goals. It took a major event to galvanize Dickinson's and the medical profession's support for Sanger.

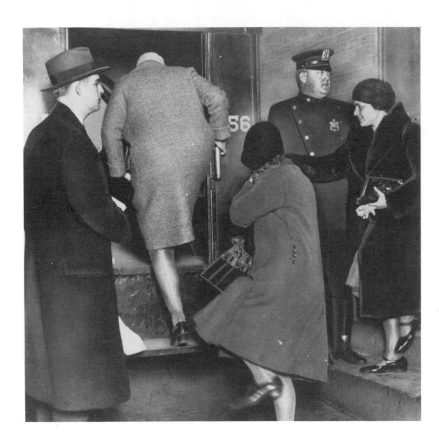

Women arrested during a police raid on the Clinical Research Bureau in April 1929 step into a police van. The raid was instigated by Catholic church officials who became alarmed by the number of Catholic women seeking birth control services.

Police Raid Brings Medical Profession's Support

The dramatic event that finally compelled the medical profession to cast its lot with the defenders of the birth control movement was triggered by the leaders of the Roman Catholic church. Catholic social workers in New York had reported to church leaders that a high percentage of Catholic women were using the services of the Clinical Research Bureau. Gravely alarmed, the archbishop of New York convinced the police to raid the clinic.

The raid took place in April 1929. Police entered the clinic on Fifteenth Street and behaved just as they had in the Brownsville raid thirteen years earlier.

They arrested doctors Hannah Stone and Elizabeth Pissoort and three nurses. They treated the patients in the waiting room like criminals. Still worse, the police removed everything they could from the clinic, including models of contraceptive devices, diaphragms, pictures, and most importantly, case records of patients who had attended the clinic.

Heywood Broun, a noted New York columnist and close personal friend of Margaret Sanger, dared the medical profession to ignore the raid. He wrote: "If the medical profession did not resent the raid, they should consult chiropractors to learn what ailed their spines."[44] The jibe was unnecessary.

In those wild, irresponsible few minutes of the raid, the police achieved what

Sanger had failed to achieve in ten years—the birth control movement gained the support of the medical profession.

A Court Trial

The New York Medical Academy, on the urging of Dr. Dickinson, acknowledged that the police had violated the legal right of privileged communication between physician and patient. In the academy's view the raid was a "grave menace to the freedom of the medical profession within

In the wake of the raid, New York writer Heywood Broun challenged the medical profession to respond.

legal qualifications for the care and treatment of their patients."[45]

Morris L. Ernst, a noted civil rights attorney and later a leading counsel for the American Civil Liberties Union, agreed to defend the doctors and nurses who were arrested in the raid. He wanted to use the case to move the court beyond the decision of the Crane case of 1918. Ernst and Sanger and her supporters wanted to use the authority of the American legal system to stand up to all those who were interfering with the birth control movement. They wanted the court to protect the legality of providing birth control information within clinics, under physician-regulated circumstances. They also wanted a ruling that the spacing of children was a legitimate medical concern.

On May 14, 1930, the case went to trial. Many circumstances were different than those of 1918. This time dozens of physicians offered to testify on behalf of Margaret Sanger and her Clinical Research Bureau. Dr. Louis T. Harris, a former New York State health commissioner, was the chief witness at the trial. He told the court: "The birth control clinic is a public health work. In preventing conception it may be said to cure because pregnancy can often be the cause of furthering the progress of disease."[46]

The presiding judge at the trial was convinced. Judge Abraham Rosenbluth reached a decision that was sympathetic to the arguments presented by Ernst and his witnesses: "If the doctor in good faith believes that the patient is a married woman, and that her health requires prevention of conception, it is no crime to so advise and instruct therein."[47]

Judge Rosenbluth also found that the New York Police Department had acted

Morris L. Ernst, attorney with the American Civil Liberties Union, defended the doctors and nurses who were arrested in the raid on the clinic.

improperly. All charges against the defendants were dropped. The Rosenbluth decision was a major victory in Margaret Sanger's crusade to bring birth control information to the women of America. Margaret Sanger announced that the decision "was one of the finest we have ever won."[48]

Church's Involvement Becomes Public

Sanger still did not know who was responsible for the raid on the clinic. She hired the Burns Detective Agency to learn the truth. The detectives found that the Roman Catholic church was behind the raid and that Archbishop Hayes had had the police gather incriminating documents against the Catholic women who had used the clinic. Sanger lost no time in publicizing this information.

Non-Catholic religious groups were alarmed that the Catholic hierarchy had used such tactics to prevent Catholics from using the services of the clinic. Many smaller religious bodies came to support Sanger and her birth control movement during 1929 and 1930. The National Council of Jewish Women, for example, endorsed the movement in 1930, as did the Unitarians and the Anglican bishops. They were followed in 1931 by the Presbyterians, the Central Conference of American Rabbis, the Universalists, and the Methodists. In 1931 the Federal Council of Churches of Christ in America—a body representing nearly twenty-three million Protestants—accepted the idea of the well-being of the family unit as central to its mission. "There is general agreement also," the Federal Council announced to its members in May 1931, "that the sex union between husbands and wives, as an expression of mutual affection without re-

The Position of the Catholic Church

Archbishop Patrick J. Hayes used his influence to prevent a discussion on the morality of birth control from taking place in New York City's town hall in 1922. The archbishop defended his actions in the following statement taken from Emily Taft Douglas's biography of Sanger.

"As a citizen and a churchman, deeply concerned with the moral well-being of our city, I feel it a public duty to protest . . . in the interest of thousands of . . . distressed mothers, who are alarmed at the daring of the advocates of birth control to bring out into an open, unrestricted, free meeting a discussion of a subject that simple prudence and decency, if not the spirit of the law, should keep within the walls of a clinic. . . . The law was enacted under the police power of the Legislature for the benefit of the morals and health of the community. . . . The law of God and man, science, public policy, human experience, are all condemnatory of birth control as preached by a few irresponsible individuals. . . .

The seventh child has been regarded traditionally with some peoples as the most favored by nature. Benjamin Franklin was the fifteenth child, John Wesley the eighteenth, Ignatius Loyola was the eighth, Catherine of Siena, one of the greatest intellectual women who ever lived, was the twenty-fourth. It has been suggested that one of the reasons for the lack of genius in our day is that we are getting the ends of the families."

Archbishop Patrick J. Hayes believed birth control was immoral.

Birth control proponents (from left to right) Dr. Sydney E. Goldstein, Henry Pratt Fairchild, Sanger, and Dr. J. Whitridge Williams after testifying before a Senate committee in Washington, D.C.

lationship to procreation, is right."[49]

The year of 1930 was exceptional for Margaret Sanger. She had helped to bring about extraordinary changes in American religious attitudes toward family planning. The synagogues and churches of America, with the exception of the Catholic church, had overcome religious tenets because they saw that strong families with fewer children offered greater hope for the perpetuation of the moral principles they expounded.

Against all odds Sanger had established a successful birth control clinic in New York, which was quickly becoming a model for the country. She had succeeded in convincing the medical profession of the importance of birth control and fami-

ly planning for the well-being of the population of the country.

Nevertheless, the Comstock Law and its statewide applications still existed. Until they were changed, many physicians and medical schools continued to avoid training in birth control concepts. Birth control paraphernalia remained expensive and scarce, even illegal in some states. Inadequate knowledge and supplies of birth control devices further limited birth control's availability. Margaret Sanger decided to take her campaign to Washington, D.C. She wanted to remove the final obstacles that controlled free discussion and the dispersal of birth control information and devices by the physicians of America.

6 Operating on a Federal Level

No true improvement in living conditions can be hoped for if the number of births be not considerably diminished.

—Minister of Finance,
the Netherlands, 1875

In 1930 Margaret Sanger decided to continue her fight for the birth control movement in Washington, D.C. There were several reasons for changing her base of operations from New York City, where she had achieved so much success, to Washington, where she was unsure of the political terrain.

On a personal level Margaret Sanger had succeeded in alienating most of the staff of the American Birth Control League. They had grown to resent her dictatorial methods, her failure to recognize their contributions, her insistence on making all decisions that were related to policies followed by the league, and her refusal to be held accountable for how she spent the funds of the organization. They disagreed with her emphasis on international birth control work. They believed that much still needed to be done in the United States. Essentially, many people had grown to oppose what they considered to be a one-woman movement.

Sanger felt that, as the leader of the American movement, she had earned the right to dominate the organization. She fundamentally opposed the league's efforts to make her more accountable. Furthermore, since her husband contributed so generously to the league, she felt she deserved complete freedom to determine how the league's funds should be spent.

While Sanger was in Europe during 1928 and 1929, the league's staff took control of the available funds of the organization and staffed the board of directors with people who believed that she had to relinquish some of her authority. Sanger returned to New York in March 1928 to confront Ellen Robertson-Jones, the acting president of the American Birth Control League. Robertson-Jones asked for compromise. Sanger refused. She resigned as president, telling the league that she was certain they would do very well without her.

Sanger knew that many of the members of the league considered her to be a fanatic but, as she observed, "what some call fanaticism is never dangerous to the life of an organization such as this one. Apathy and languid convictions are."[50] With Sanger's departure and the related termination of Noah Slee's financial support, the American Birth Control League never recovered its former importance.

Break with the American Birth Control League

The American Birth Control League gave respectability to the birth control movement. When Margaret Sanger broke with the league in 1929, she justified her action in this excerpt from her Autobiography:

"Regretfully I found the League was to side-step the greatest and most far-reaching opportunity yet offered it. It was logically equipped to enter the legislative field. But it wanted to progress state by state. I was convinced action in the Federal sphere would be quicker and much much broader educationally, and that, furthermore, success there would provide a precedent for the states.

When you build an organization, you try to combine harmonious elements, but you cannot tell what they will turn out to be until a certain interval has elapsed. Some of these women were in the movement for reasons they themselves did not always understand. A few liked the sensation of being important and having personal attention; they were at their best in following an individual, yet I never felt they were doing it for me. The liberals who had started with me had never demanded reward. What they gave was for the cause; they refused to work for people; they worked with them or not at all.

Those who disagreed with me believed the emphasis should be on social register membership, and argued that my associations had been radical."

Undermining the Comstock Law

Margaret Sanger's primary battle in 1930 was a direct confrontation with the Comstock Law. For her, undermining the Comstock Law was the key to future progress.

Sanger believed that no further advances in birth control could be made in the United States until the 1873 legislation was eliminated. While the 1918 Crane and 1930 Rosenbluth decisions permitted physicians to discuss birth control with their patients, the Comstock Law still stood in the way of the sale and availability of inexpensive and effective birth control methods.

Businesspeople were still afraid to manufacture birth control devices in the United States for fear of federal prosecution. Sanger and her husband had even encouraged a friend to start a business called the Holland-Rantos Company. It successfully produced a limited number of diaphragms, but never enough to supply the needs of the American population.

The Comstock Law forbade the importation of diaphragms from Europe. Very few druggists had the courage to defy the law and obtain these devices.

In order, therefore, to supply American needs, the birth control movement had gone into the business of smuggling. Wealthy people who supported the movement would smuggle as many diaphragms as possible into the country when they returned from their summer trips to Europe. They called the league headquarters in New York City and announced: "Just back from England. Please send someone over for the jewels."[51]

Noah Slee, Margaret Sanger's second husband, also participated in smuggling. He used his firm's Three-In-One oil plant in Montreal, Canada, as a base for a smug-

gling operation. Diaphragms, tightly packed together in oil cans, were shipped across the border to Slee's plant in Rahway, New Jersey. From there thousands were moved to the Clinical Research Bureau in New York City.

In spite of these successful smuggling methods, there were still insufficient birth control devices to meet the needs of the American market. Margaret Sanger decided once and for all to take on the Comstock laws directly. She no longer had an organizational base in New York City, so she set up an office in Washington, D.C., where she could be close to the forces she would have to influence.

She created a new organization—the National Committee on Federal Legislation for Birth Control. It operated some-

Through her new organization, the National Committee on Federal Legislation for Birth Control, Sanger and her staff raised money and lobbied legislators in an effort to overturn the Comstock Law.

what like a modern PAC (political action committee), or lobbying organization. It was designed to raise money and to put pressure on legislators to overturn the Comstock Law.

Sanger brought a few of her faithful followers to Washington. They included Frances Brooks Ackerman, Ida Timme, and Katharine Houghton Hepburn.

From her headquarters and with her small but dependable staff, Sanger developed a nationwide organization of many field-workers. These field-workers put pressure on local representatives to support the repeal of the Comstock Law. They passed out petitions. They went to local meetings of all sorts—labor, church, political—to get names on petitions to send to legislators in Washington.

These grass roots, or local, efforts made the National Committee a very effective voice in American affairs. Margaret Sanger issued directives to her field-workers all over the country to gather signatures and collect funds. Almost immediately the state and local birth control organizations were implementing her directives. At one point she had the support of organizations representing approximately twelve million American women.

The Doctors Only Bill

Meanwhile, in Washington, D.C., Margaret Sanger and her staff carried out a campaign of pressure directed toward any legislator whom they believed had the least sympathy for their cause. They telephoned legislators' staff members to gain their support for the proposed legislation. They wrote memoranda to remind legislators of the importance of the birth control movement. Margaret and her colleagues sat outside the offices of influential members of Congress in an attempt to get a congressional author for their bill, the Doctors Only Bill.

The intent of the Doctors Only Bill was simple: to extract the remaining teeth from the Comstock Law. The Doctors Only Bill would make it legal for doctors to send contraceptive information through the mails, to obtain imported birth control materials without fear of prosecution, to instruct students in birth control techniques, and to conduct research and publish materials on birth control technology. In addition, clinic doctors would be able to freely advise patients re-

Sanger prepares her Senate testimony on the Doctors Only Bill.

Fearing a political backlash, Senator Hattie Caraway of Arkansas declined to sponsor the Doctors Only Bill.

had to give up two Congressmen now because we don't have enough people. If New York wants to wipe out her population, she can. We need ours."[53] Unwise in the ways of Washington, Sanger repeatedly approached the wrong people in her efforts to find a sponsor for her proposal.

She finally convinced Senator Henry D. Hatfield of West Virginia to sponsor the bill in 1932. It was also introduced in the House of Representatives by Frank Hancock of North Carolina. But it made little progress.

In 1934 Sanger renewed her efforts to promote the Doctors Only Bill. This time it actually passed out of committee and was voted on by the full House of Representatives. But at the very last moment, Senator Pat McCarren, a Catholic senator

At Sanger's urging, Senator Henry D. Hatfield of West Virginia agreed to sponsor the bill.

garding the availability of all types of birth control devices. They could also advertise that such information was available at their clinics.

If the Doctors Only Bill passed through Congress, the federal laws restricting contraceptive information would be dead. But it was not easy to find a sponsor for the bill. Hattie Caraway, the first woman senator, declined the honor. She indicated that although she was in favor of Mrs. Sanger's efforts, "her own secretary would not let her touch it."[52]

Sanger next approached Richard B. Russell of Georgia. He was the father of eighteen children by two wives. His response to her request indicated that the issues raised by the proposed legislation were too political. Russell told Sanger: "We don't need birth control in Georgia. We've from Reno, Nevada, asked to have it recalled to its original committee for further review. There it died.

Future Leads to Success

That was as close as Margaret Sanger ever came to ridding the law books of the hated Comstock regulations. Although cases have rarely been prosecuted, most of the Comstock laws still remain. While Sanger's legislative efforts failed, the birth control movement achieved a major victory in 1937 that made the Comstock laws virtually irrelevant.

During a trip to Zurich, Switzerland, Margaret Sanger had been contacted by a representative of a Japanese company called Majimi. The salesman indicated that his company had diaphragms available for international sale. Sanger decided that the time had come to test the importation sections of the Comstock legislation in the courts. She placed a larger order for the products and instructed that the package be sent to Dr. Elizabeth M. Stone, the medical director of the Clinical Research Bureau.

When the package, clearly marked as containing diaphragms, arrived at U.S. Customs, it was confiscated and destroyed under Section 305 of the Revenue Act. This barred pornographic materials from entering the United States.

Margaret Sanger placed another order which also was confiscated. She and her lawyers then took the case to court. They argued that the Comstock laws, in preventing the importation of birth control devices, interfered with the medical relationship between physicians and their patients.

The resulting court contest came to be

American Women's Association Supports Sanger

Sanger's legislative efforts caught the attention of the American Women's Association, who awarded her their annual prize in 1931. In this excerpt taken from David M. Kennedy's book, the association notes that:

"[Sanger] has fought a battle against almost every influence which in the past was considered necessary to the success of a cause. Against her stood the state, the church, the schools, the press and society. She has fought that battle singlehanded . . . a pioneer of pioneers.

She has carried her cause without remuneration or personal reward other than poverty, condemnation and ostracism. She has changed and is changing the entire social structure of our world. She has opened the doors of knowledge and thereby given light, freedom and happiness to thousands caught in the tragic meshes of ignorance. She is remaking the world."

known as the One Package Case. The case came to trial in December 1935 and was heard by Judge Grover Moscowitz in the U.S. District Court for southern New York. After listening to arguments on both sides, Judge Moscowitz ordered that the offending items be delivered to Dr. Stone. In Moscowitz's view, the court "could not assume that Congress intended to interfere with doctors prescribing for the health of the people."[54]

The state of New York immediately appealed the case because of the revolutionary implications of Moscowitz's decision. The appeals case was heard in 1936 by Judge Augustus N. Hand of the Circuit Court of Appeals. Judge Hand upheld the decision of the lower court. He found that the design of the Comstock Law "in our opinion, was not to prevent the importation, sale or carriage by mail of things which might intelligently be employed by conscientious and competent physicians for the purpose of saving lives or promoting the well-being of their patients."[55] Margaret Sanger and her supporters called the decision "the greatest victory in birth control history."[56] The decision reached in the One Package Case brought about the effective demise of the Comstock Law. The American judiciary system essentially overruled the American legislative system in this matter. What Sanger could not win in Congress, she won in the courts.

Dr. Elizabeth Stone, medical director of the Clinical Research Bureau, emphasized the importance of Judge Hand's decision. She wrote in 1937 that the judiciary "once and for all established contraception as a recognized part of medical practice and removed the last legal barriers to the dissemination of contraceptive knowledge."[57]

Companies could now freely import birth control devices. American companies began to produce birth control devices of high quality. An entirely new industry began to blossom in the United States. During the Great Depression the manufacture of birth control devices was the one area of American industry that showed a dramatic growth curve.

The decision also affected the field of gynecology. For example, in 1930 only thirteen of the top seventy-five medical schools in the country offered regular courses in contraception. By 1937 about half of these schools had begun to teach the subject. More physicians attended programs sponsored by the Clinical Research Bureau. They brought important information back to their own practices and to their professional societies.

Even the American Medical Association (AMA) showed active and public support for birth control. At its annual conference in 1937 the AMA openly endorsed birth control for the first time as an important aspect of family medicine. The AMA organized national committees to develop innovative approaches to help women plan the spacing of their families.

Margaret Sanger had achieved unimaginable success by 1937. She had helped to free American women from the ill effects of unplanned pregnancies. She had opened a frank discussion of sexual issues.

Bringing Birth Control to Rural America

Another individual might have taken time off to rest and bask in her triumphant success. But long before the One Package decision, Margaret Sanger was involved in yet another dramatic project. She wanted to make birth control a public health responsibility of the states in the country. She knew that the federal government made funds available to the states to be used for mother-and-children health issues. Sanger wanted birth control to be recognized as such an issue. In this way, federal money could be made available to the rural poor people of the country.

There was a great need. Rural America was largely unaffected by the birth control battles of the previous decade. The movement had developed largely as an urban campaign. Yet the need for information was just as acute in the rural south and west as it was in the cities. At the height of the Great Depression in particular, the need for birth control information became critical. That was because the birth rate soared during this period and poverty in rural areas became more severe than ever. Yet, few medical facilities were available to these people.

Margaret Sanger decided to carry on her work among the rural poor through the education department of her Clinical Research Bureau. She also used the field staff who had worked on behalf of the Doctors Only Bill in Congress to carry birth control information into rural areas of the country. Her urgency to get out the word about birth control is conveyed in her message to her field staff: "There are today approximately 320 birth control centers in America. I look forward to seeing not twice that number but ten times that number at the close of 1937."[58]

Her staff was instructed to offer information wherever it could be used to help in rural communities. In particular they should make contact with public health agencies and public health doctors. Hospitals, relief agencies, and public health offices all received visits from Sanger's field staff, who provided information on how to help poor people in family planning.

Sanger personally visited many rural sites. She traveled to the migrant camps of Oklahoma to help rural women learn about birth control. She brought information and inspiration to women who never

With the battle against the Comstock laws virtually won, Sanger shifted her focus to bringing contraceptive information to rural America. She made many personal visits to Oklahoma farm families and others during the 1930s.

Sanger enlisted the help of Eleanor Roosevelt in obtaining federal money for birth control programs.

before had considered the possibility of limiting the size of their families.

She also tried to get the new federal agencies set up during the depression to assist in her efforts. Here she met the active opposition of many government administrators. People such as Katherine Lenroot of the federal Children's Bureau, for example, refused to release desperately needed funds to provide birth control information. There may have been some fear on the part of such people that a successful birth control movement would eliminate the need for their bureaus.

Margaret Sanger refused to be stopped by such administrators. She had found ways to get around them in the past. This time she enlisted the support of Eleanor Roosevelt, wife of the president of the United States. Mrs. Roosevelt, warmly, if cautiously, helped apply pressure that released the Children's Bureau funds. By this act the government demonstrated support for maternal and child welfare programs, including cautious support for birth control programs.

All these successes—in the courts, in the medical profession, in the development of outreach programs through rural clinics, and in the Children's Bureau made Sanger something of a folk hero. In 1930 the distinguished American educator, John Dewey, said of Margaret Sanger, "When we look at the work she has done, I think we can begin to understand what that passage in the New Testament means about faith moving mountains." [59]

In 1932 she was honored by the American Women's Association, a national professional woman's group, for her efforts in Washington to defeat the Comstock Law. In awarding Sanger their medal of achievement, the organization announced:

> She has fought a battle against almost every influence which in the past was considered necessary to the success of a cause. Against her stood the state, the Church, the schools, the press and society. She has fought those battles single handed, a pioneer of pioneers. [60]

In 1937 she received the New York City Town Hall Association Medal for her work on behalf of women.

Sanger's enormous successes in the United States were only a partial fulfillment of her vision. Sanger also believed that she must bring her campaign for women's reproductive freedom to the rest of the world.

Chapter 7
Bigger Worlds and Other Fights

Man was godlike in the planned breeding of plants and animals but rabbitlike in the unplanned breeding of ourselves.

—Arnold Toynbee

During the course of her long life, Margaret Sanger traveled abroad a great deal. At times she was away from the United States for over a year. This extensive international experience made her aware—more than most people active in the birth control movement—of the unique characteristics and needs of people in different parts of the world. She also learned that national population policies could be based on political rather than social or economic considerations.

During these travels she was continuously on the lookout for more information, for additional techniques, and for breakthroughs that would reduce the burden of unwanted pregnancies and help keep the population in line with the food supply.

Her trip to Germany in 1920 is illustrative of her almost fanatical devotion to the birth control movement. She went because she had heard rumors that a new, easily dispensed spermicidal jelly had been developed in that country. She traced the rumor from Berlin to Dresden, from Dresden to Munich, and finally to

Friedrichshafen, where she found a chemist who had developed the compound.

She arranged to obtain a supply of the jelly. Chemists, working at the Clinical Research Bureau, later improved upon the original product. Margaret Sanger began discussing its value for women during her many speaking tours in Europe and America.

During this same trip Margaret Sanger began to notice that even though German scientists were developing new birth control technology, German nationalists were extolling the virtues of large families. Sanger wrote a letter to a friend in the United States describing this troubling development. She believed that the Germans wanted to create powerful armies to avenge Germany's honor and, according to Sanger, "treated their women like nothing more than breeding stock."[61] She also described seeing women yoked like draft animals, pulling plows through the fields. She heard militarist speeches by German leaders that she believed degraded females by referring to women as reproductive mechanisms for the state.

Sanger decided to ask some German physicians what they thought about birth control. She was shocked by the reply. "Nein, Nein! No birth control in Germany! It is abortions here only. With abortions it is all in our hands. Never will Germany give control of its population to women. Never will it let women control the race."[62] What she learned was that the Germans were ferociously hostile "to attempts by the 'fit' [Aryan] either to practice contraception or to abort."[63]

A Trip to Asia

Sanger's trip to Asia in 1921 made her realize still more dramatically the impediments that stood in the way of the international birth control movement. Her friend Baroness Shidzue Ishimoto asked her to speak before a group of Japanese independent thinkers called the Kaizo. The Kaizo had extended this invitation to only three other people—Bertrand Russell, Albert Einstein, and H.G. Wells. The group's invitation to Margaret Sanger indicated her growing international reputation. Accompanied by her son Grant and Noah Slee, she set sail for Japan.

At first it was not certain that she would even be able to get into the country. The Japanese government had denied her a visa while she was still in the United States. When she arrived nonetheless, carrying only a Chinese visa, the Japanese authorities in Tokyo tried to prevent her from landing. There was concern in official circles that her presence might cause a disturbance. Finally the British authorities in Tokyo agreed to intervene on her behalf, and she was permitted to land. But she had to agree not to cause any trouble while she was in Tokyo.

In Japan Sanger gave many public speeches about population control. Members of the Japanese Medical Association, the Tokyo Chamber of Commerce, and the YMCA of Tokyo eagerly listened to her talks. She emphasized the importance of family planning and family spacing to help insure the health of the human race. Everywhere she went, crowds of reporters followed. Her ideas were discussed in the Japanese newspapers.

Her speeches touched a very sensitive topic. The Japanese population was increasing dramatically in the 1920s. One million Japanese babies were born every year. Twenty-six hundred Japanese lived on each square mile of arable land. In

Sanger and her son Grant prepare to set sail for Japan. Sanger spoke to many Japanese groups about family planning and population control.

Baroness Shidzue Ishimoto (left) invited Sanger (right) to speak before an elite group of Japanese intellectuals called the Kaizo.

England, by contrast, the comparable figure was 466 people to a square mile.

Sanger viewed this situation as unhealthy for mothers and their babies and degrading to the human spirit. "Men and women of Japan," she begged, "I appeal to you to make your women something more than breeding machines."[64] But her appeal contradicted the policies of Japan's more militaristic elements. They, like their counterparts in Germany, spoke openly in the 1920s of conquering new lands to feed the Japanese population and of finding additional living space in which to house it.

Margaret Sanger visited factories where little girls worked in slavelike conditions. She saw the crowded slums of Tokyo and the district of the child prostitutes. She was filled with a desire to help the women of Japan control the growth of population that she believed was causing

these horrors.

If Japan's population was not controlled, Sanger believed, its explosion would lead to war. In her speeches she did not hesitate to warn the Japanese that uncontrolled population growth endangered their own survival and that of their neighbors.

Because of her outspokenness, Sanger's Japanese hosts were concerned for her safety. Some members of the Kaizo group feared that she might even be physically attacked. They felt a sense of relief when she traveled on to China.

China

In Shanghai she saw tragic scenes of human want and degradation that were every bit as pitiful as those she had observed

China's Unwanted Children

Sanger describes in her Autobiography *the methods available to poor Chinese to deal with excess children:*

"The only method of family limitation known to the poor Chinese was infanticide of girl babies by suffocation or drowning. The Chinese had so low a margin of subsistence that, if the law forbade them to dispose of one child, another was starved out. Sometimes two little girls had to be sold to keep one boy alive; in dire necessity even he might have to be parted with to some sonless man who wanted to ensure ancestor worship. But because the elder girls could begin to help in the fields or become servants in some rich landowner's household, usually it was the three and four year olds who were turned over to brothels. There they stayed until mature enough to be set to working out their indenture. If they ever tried unsuccessfully to find freedom, the proprietors might beat them unmercifully, sometimes even breaking their legs so that they could not walk, much less ever run away again."

in Japan. Thousands of female infants were sold into bondage to be raised as prostitutes. The population was so large and food so scarce that families, trying to survive, became ruthless in the exploitation of unwanted female children.

Sanger saw a woman lying in the street and thought that she was dying. Instead, it turned out that the woman was a leper giving birth in the middle of a crowd, which had gathered to watch. It was "so meaningless an incident in this nation of rampant breeding" she recalled, "that not one of the onlookers took the effort to call for help."[65]

These sights and impressions became central to her thinking and writing in the 1920s and 1930s. She wrote in January 1922 for example, that "the greatest threat to the peace of the world is to be found in the teeming population of Asia."[66] She feared that aggressive countries with large populations would take over the territory of other countries in order to feed their own people. She warned people in the United States about what she had seen in Germany and in Japan. At a gathering at the Commodore Hotel in New York, she observed that "birth control must save the world from another and more devastating holocaust" because she saw war as the only possible outcome of unchecked population growth.[67] Thus, she was convinced that birth control was not only a woman's issue, but also critical to the survival of the human race. She re-

A Disturbing Incident in China

During her visit to China, Margaret Sanger witnessed scenes of human despair and suffering, which she described in her Autobiography:

"It amazed me to see that foreigners could be so near and yet close their eyes to the wretched, degrading conditions of devastating squalor in the native quarters [of Peking near the foreign embassies]. Once while a missionary was guiding me through the Chinese City, we noted a crowd, children included, gathered in curiosity around a leper woman. She was on the ground, sighing and breathing heavily. Nobody offered to help her. 'Maybe she's dying,' said my companion. Just then the woman gave a fearful groan and took a baby from under her rags. She knew what to do, manipulated her thighs and abdomen, got the afterbirth, bit the cord with her teeth, put the baby aside, turned over, and rested. No trace of emotion showed on the faces of the watchers."

In a letter to Sanger, English economist John Maynard Keynes wrote that he believed population was both an economic and political problem.

peated this theme again and again in hundreds of speeches in the next several years.

Margaret Sanger's many friends in England and elsewhere encouraged her to continue her battle. Havelock Ellis, H.G. Wells, George Bernard Shaw, and many other prominent figures appreciated her personal strength and determination. More importantly, she shared a common vision with these writers. They believed that birth control was the key to preventing the world from destroying itself through uncontrolled population growth and nationalistic expansion. For example, John Maynard Keynes, the great English economist, wrote a letter to Sanger in which he declared that "population was not only an economic problem but would soon be recognized as the greatest of all political questions."[68]

Plans for an International Conference

Sanger made every effort to attend as many international conferences on the subject of birth control as possible. In 1922 she was at the London Birth Control Conference, along with representatives from most of the European countries. The delegates applauded Sanger's singular efforts to make birth control a topic of serious discussion in the United States and Japan. In fact, they recognized Margaret Sanger as the greatest pioneer of the modern movement. She, in turn, saw the importance of American and European activists interacting and pooling their re-sources. What better way than to hold an international conference in the United States?

She had inadequate funds. Her American colleagues in the movement did not support her international efforts. She had many other obligations. Nevertheless, she forged ahead, found the money, and organized the Sixth International Neo-Malthusian and Birth Control Conference in New York City in 1925.

It was an enormous success. The eight hundred delegates from eighteen countries lent credibility to the vitality of the international birth control movement. Most importantly, the hundreds of professional papers presented underscored the relationship between birth control issues and world population concerns. This connec-

Although short on funds, Sanger organized the Sixth International Neo-Malthusian and Birth Control Conference in New York City in 1925. Sanger (center) appears here with board members.

tion had never before been made in a world forum.

The conference also provided an opportunity for physicians to meet in closed sessions. Doctors Stone and Cooper of the Clinical Research Bureau discussed advances the clinic had made in birth control techniques. This session was part of Margaret Sanger's campaign to enlist American physicians in the cause of reproductive choice and in understanding its international implications. She hoped that physicians would be impressed by the clinic's success in improving the health of its patients. Some physicians might even become advocates for birth control on a national or even international level, she thought.

The audience wanted statistics and information about birth control devices. They were not disappointed. Doctors Stone and Cooper drew their material from the records of the first eleven hundred patients treated at the Clinical Research Bureau in New York City. They pro-

vided information on birth control studies and techniques that the American medical profession was otherwise unable to obtain. And since the information was provided within the confines of a scientific meeting, the New York Police Department dared not intervene. Clearly this previously unavailable information "was the sensation of the conference."[69]

Sanger brought together international experts, and she linked the birth control movement with the issue of international peace. She packaged this all within the framework of science and made birth control a rational issue for the skeptical thinker.

At the conclusion of the conference the delegates tried to elect Margaret Sanger as the international president of the movement. She was deeply touched by their support, but she understood the importance of having a scientist head the movement. So they selected Dr. C.C. Little of the University of Michigan instead. The delegates also agreed to establish an inter-

Members of the world population conference held in Geneva, Switzerland in 1927. The relationship between population growth and food supply was one of many topics discussed.

Among the many speakers at the conference was Julian Huxley.

national birth control information center in London.

Margaret Sanger was inspired by the success of the Sixth International Conference. She also was so fearful of the growing militarism in Germany, Italy, and Japan that she took a step she had tried to avoid. She involved herself in international politics.

A Conference in Geneva

Sanger began to organize another international conference on birth control to be held in Geneva, Switzerland. Geneva was selected because the League of Nations was headquartered there. Margaret Sanger hoped to organize a successful conference that would compel the international organization to put population

An International Influence

In 1952 at the age of sixty-eight, Margaret Sanger went to India to attend an Indian Birth Control Conference. Dr. C.P. Blacker, a delegate from England, described Mrs. Sanger's performance at this time in this speech taken from Madeline Gray's work.

"Mrs. Sanger was wonderfully responsive to her audiences. She could draw from them as much as she gave them. . . . Large assemblages acted on her like a tonic. She visibly drew strength and zest from the packed seats and galleries; and the iller she seemed beforehand the more triumphant was her performance.

Her charm and warmth . . . have been abundantly stressed. What I would particularly like to mention is her power of strategical thinking. She saw how Asia, Europe, and America could play different but complementary roles. This grand design, by no means obvious at the start, is now so taken for granted that it can easily be forgotten that Mrs. Sanger was its originator and architect."

control on its official agenda.

Catholic countries opposed Sanger's leading role in the organization of the conference, so she worked without her name on the program itself. She brought in prominent speakers, such as John Maynard Keynes and Julian Huxley, who were concerned with population issues. Demographers, biologists, economists, and Socialists met in seminars. Sir Bernard Mallet, a former president of England's Royal Statistical Society, accepted Sanger's invitation to serve as chairman of the conference. Apart from his vast knowledge of population statistics, Mallet had been selected for another reason. Sanger knew that he was a close friend of Sir Eric Drummond, the secretary general of the League of Nations, whose support on population control matters was vital for the movement.

The conference provided the world scientific community with an enormous amount of information on how unchecked population growth affected the world's food supply. The delegates also discussed Germany's and Japan's attempts to encourage population growth for nationalistic and aggressive purposes. The conference condemned such expansion and emphasized the need for stringent birth control methods to relieve the pressure of populations on the environment.

On to India

In 1935 Margaret Sanger received an invitation to visit India. India had a population whose growth appeared to outstrip its food supply. Mrs. Sanger was asked to attend an All-India Women's Conference,

which had endorsed the idea of birth control as a key to dealing with India's economic and social woes.

While she was in India, Mrs. Sanger visited with Mahatma Gandhi, who had recently resigned from his position in the India National Congress. She also met with Mme. Vijaya Lakshmi Pandit, a future president of the United Nations General Assembly. Pandit was receptive to her ideas; Gandhi was not. Gandhi condemned the sexual relationship between husband and wife. The sixty-six-year-old Gandhi's method of birth control was total abstinence, which he had been practicing since the age of thirty-eight.

This ascetic approach to the problem of the world's growing population ran

Vijaya Lakshmi Pandit (left) was receptive to Sanger's ideas about using birth control to help solve India's economic and social problems.

Sanger meets Mahatma Gandhi. The two disagreed on the issue of population control: Gandhi favored abstinence while Sanger favored other methods.

counter to Sanger's own beliefs and personal behavior. She believed that sexual satisfaction played a major role in marital happiness. Gandhi's views remained a mystery to her. More importantly, she certainly did not believe that asceticism held much promise as a means of addressing the worldwide population explosion.

Despite her ideological differences with Gandhi, Sanger's Indian voyage was productive. She gained new insight into the complexity of the world population explosion. She realized that her cause would be hampered in countries like India, which lacked medical facilities. This meant that the traditional birth control techniques she advocated could not be used widely in nonindustrial countries. There were insufficient doctors, clinics, nurses, and equipment. Sanger came away from the experience acutely conscious of yet another aspect to the problem of birth control.

World War II temporarily interrupted Sanger's international campaign, but she resumed her efforts after 1945. In 1946 she went to Stockholm, Sweden, to work with the Swedish birth control advocate Elise Ottesen-Jensen. The two women planned a new international conference that took place in Cheltenham, England in 1948. The Cheltenham conference was an enormous success.

Sir John Boyd-Orr, director general of the United Nations Food and Agricultural Organization, was the main speaker. The speech by Boyd-Orr marked the active involvement and commitment of the United Nations to the world's population crisis. The delegates agreed that the crisis was a

Sir John Boyd-Orr's speech at the international conference in Cheltenham marked the entry of the United Nations in the population growth debate.

result of the world's population growing faster than was the means to feed it. Sanger believed it could be managed only through the work of an international organization. Boyd-Orr's speech, which addressed the role of the United Nations in birth control, was a realization of another of Margaret Sanger's dreams.

Banned from Japan

With that success behind her, Margaret Sanger, now ill at age seventy-one, eagerly resumed her personal efforts to influence the international community to encourage birth control programs. She was particularly concerned that Japan, battered by World War II losses, would try to increase its own population.

She decided to visit some of her Japanese friends. Gen. Douglas MacArthur, who was the commander of the American occupation forces, refused to grant her an entry visa in 1950. Of a country of 79 million people, 180,000 Japanese Catholics had influenced MacArthur to keep the troublemaker out.

After MacArthur was relieved of his command, the situation changed. In 1951 Margaret Sanger made her visit to Japan and was warmly welcomed by a population clamoring for birth control information. Despite being weakened by heart ailments, Sanger delivered several addresses, one of them to eight hundred people. At the age of seventy-three she still enthusiastically instructed doctors and nurse midwives on the latest contraceptive devices.

The triumphant visit to Japan was followed by still another trip to Sweden, where in 1953 she was elected president of

Indian prime minister Nehru shares a few words with Sanger. Sanger was impressed by Nehru, calling him the "greatest living statesman" in the world.

the International Birth Control Federation. After that, Sanger made three more trips to Japan.

Finally she made a last trip to New Delhi, India, in 1959. Along with Lady Rama Rau, president of the Family Planning Association of India, Sanger, now age eighty, served as cosponsor of a 750-delegate International Family Planning Conference.

Margaret Sanger described the event to her granddaughter, Peggy:

Yesterday was a great and joyous day for me. The conference was opened by Prime Minister Nehru who bent over me and said, "It is wonderful that you came to us from so far away." He then offered me his arm, and together we walked out into the Great Auditorium facing hundreds of camera shots and news men. I had to speak from the platform and said, "Mr. Nehru is the greatest living statesman in all this world." It was a great victory for our Cause, and I am happy that I came.[70]

At the conclusion of the conference the delegates voted Margaret Sanger president emeritus for life of the International Planned Parenthood Federation in recognition of her contributions to the cause of birth control education.

By this time Sanger was quite frail. She did not have many more years left to live. Yet she knew that her final crusade on behalf of the birth control movement was about to come to fruition. Even as she spoke in New Delhi, trial runs of a chemical birth control method were taking place in Puerto Rico and in the United States.

Chapter
8 Contributions

Margaret Sanger's name will go down in history as one of the company of pioneers who have not been afraid to do what was to be done. Such men and women live in the life of humanity to come.

—Pearl Buck

For many years Margaret Sanger thought about a chemical means of contraception. Her back-road trips through America and visits to the developing regions of the world convinced her of the importance of finding an inexpensive, safe, and efficient method of birth control to replace the diaphragm.

The diaphragm was time consuming to fit and to maintain. Because it required a doctor's consultation, it was difficult for women in underdeveloped and poor countries to use. These characteristics put it out of the reach of most of the world's women. Yet, a substitute for the diaphragm remained elusive. Sanger's own Clinical Research Bureau scientists had experimented with various chemical compounds but had not found the right formula.

Then an exciting early research breakthrough occurred in 1936. Dr. Carl C. Hartman published a book called *The Ovulation in Women.* Hartman demonstrated the role of hormones in determining the periodic, monthly cycle of fertile and infertile periods in human females. With this knowledge, researchers tried to find a way to interfere with women's fertile periods in order to prevent conception.

After 1945 scientists began studies with progesterone. Progesterone is a female hormone secretion that is triggered by ovulation. Researchers hoped that work with the female hormone would result in a chemical birth control method.

On the Search for an Oral Contraceptive

Margaret Sanger was already in her late sixties when she began to pursue the elusive oral contraceptive. Upon the death of her husband, Noah Slee, Sanger received enough funds to begin work on her project. She was assisted in this effort by her old friend Katherine Dexter McCormick.

McCormick was married to the son of Stanley McCormick, the heir to the McCormick International Harvester fortune. McCormick was a very unusual woman. Many years before, she had been one of the first women to earn a degree from Massachusetts Institute of Technology. As a trained biologist she was always interest-

98 ■ THE IMPORTANCE OF MARGARET SANGER

Finding the Right Physician

These fund-raising efforts, along with the two women's own contributions, succeeded in securing the necessary seed money (start-up money) for a major research project. The money was used to support the work of an organization called the Worcester Foundation for Experimental Biology located in Massachusetts.

Dr. Gregory Pincus, a biologist who had earned a reputation as an expert on reproduction, worked at the foundation. In the early 1950s Dr. Pincus was studying steroid hormones. In the 1930s, however, he had conducted reproductive research on rabbits and had been able to stop ovu-

Dr. Gregory Pincus firmly established the connection between ovulation and conception. His work ultimately led to the development of the birth control pill.

Katherine Dexter McCormick joined forces with Sanger to raise money for research into development of an oral contraceptive.

ed in scientific projects. When Sanger turned to McCormick to help raise the enormous sums that would be necessary to conduct the research to produce an oral contraceptive, her friend was interested and willing to help.

The two women combined their unique talents in the effort to raise money to begin the project. McCormick entertained the Rockefellers, Eleanor Roosevelt, and other distinguished people in her Santa Barbara, California, home. She invited Sanger to speak at these gatherings in order to enlist the financial support of McCormick's friends.

lation. His experimental rabbits had become infertile, thereby establishing a clear connection between ovulation and conception.

In 1950 Sanger and McCormick consulted Dr. Pincus and discussed their goal of finding a pill that could control fertility. Dr. Pincus was excited by the financial support offered for his research but had several reservations. He warned the two women that he needed a tremendous amount of money for the research, which he knew would take more than several years to complete. Also, he needed the collaboration of a physician. Pincus believed that the public might discount the work of a biologist and would more readily accept the efforts of a physician in the area of birth control technology.

Discussions then took place with Dr. John Rock, who was chief of obstetrics and gynecology at Harvard University Medical School. Dr. Rock was Catholic and was somewhat reluctant to become involved in Dr. Pincus's research. Eventually, however, he agreed to work quietly with Pincus on the project.

The concern of these scientists was that the Catholic community in Massachusetts, only one of two states that had laws against the use of contraceptives, might interfere with the work of the foundation. But with Margaret Sanger still working actively to fund their research, Dr. Rock finally came out openly in 1954 in support of the project. He even con-

A Fear of Publicity

When an article appeared in 1952 in Look magazine suggesting the possibility that Pincus and Rock might be developing a birth control pill, Sanger asked the National Director of Planned Parenthood that such information be kept secret. This excerpt is taken from Madeline Gray's book.

"Instead of giving me joy to see the preliminary publicity, I know that so many things can happen until there is an actual accomplishment and thorough testing of these mythical drugs, that I am worried stiff.

As to the amazing and wonderful news of the "Pill," may I again beg of you to get in direct contact with the American Medical Association before you give out anything to any other group? They can kill the best idea in the world, even more decidedly than the Catholics. With all the wealth of Hutton who bought the Carol Dankin formula and standardized it into Zonite, he made an enemy of the A.M.A. only because he did not submit his facts to Chicago before he went to the general public. To this day the M.D.'s are against Zonite, knowing it is far better on tissues and membranes than Lysol. So please ask or invite the official A.M.A. to come in on the kill!"

ducted some tests at his own clinic in Brookline, Massachusetts.

The research conducted at the Worcester Foundation dealt with ways to stop production of mature egg cells in women. The result was "the Pill." This was the long-awaited safe, discrete, affordable, and accessible contraceptive. And it was soon ready for testing. All that was necessary were the funds to conduct the expensive testing process. But because the Pill was so controversial, it was difficult to obtain funding from the usual scientific sources.

Once again Sanger and her connections came to the rescue of yet another critical development in birth control. Again it was McCormick who provided the necessary money. Upon the death of her husband, McCormick came into possession of fifteen million dollars. She immediately contacted Sanger, and together the two elderly women went to meet Dr. Rock

Dr. John Rock is credited with the development of the birth control pill. He began his efforts at the request of Gregory Pincus. "The Pill" provided women with a safe, discrete, affordable, and accessible method of birth control.

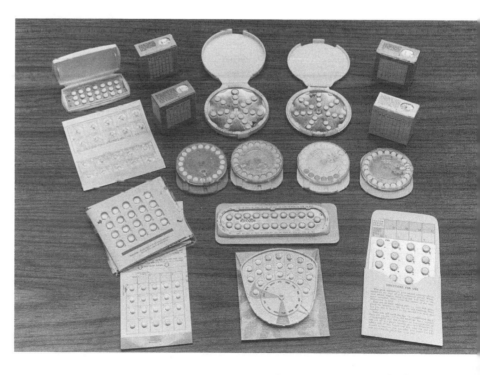

They offered him the sum of forty-five thousand dollars a year for five years to begin his testing. They told Dr. Rock that more money would be available later to complete the work.

Thanks to the efforts of Margaret Sanger and her fund-raising ability, the testing phase of the Pill continued uninterrupted. Sanger and McCormick never suspected that the entire process would take ten years and cost over two million dollars to complete.

Women in Puerto Rico, Haiti, and Los Angeles volunteered to take part in the testing of the oral contraceptive. There were extensive checks and reviews of the process. In fact, the Pill "was more widely tested than any drug in history."[71] After this extensive testing phase, the federal Food and Drug Administration gave its approval for use of the Pill in 1960. The compound was marketed under the trade name of Enovid. A representative of the C.D. Searle drug company, which did much of the research, said that "the introduction of the birth control pill in 1960 can be seen as the climax of the family planning movement."[72] Sanger's dream had come true. A safe, effective, socially acceptable contraceptive was available to American women.

The Draper Report

Sanger now wanted the American government to play a role in controlling world population growth. She hoped that President Dwight D. Eisenhower would step forward on behalf of this cause. Certainly the Draper Report should have acted as a stimulus.

Gen. William H. Draper had been involved in some of the government's recent work on world population growth. He had been asked to head a federal commission that was to assess the value of foreign aid given by the United States to underdeveloped countries. The Draper Report indicated that the populations of many countries were growing so quickly that the growth offset the value of any aid extended by the United States. If curbs were not placed on the increase in the growth of the world's population, the human crisis would be enormous.

President Eisenhower decided to ignore the report, in large part because of protests by American Catholic leaders. The eighty-year-old Sanger was outraged that once again religion interfered with what

A commission headed by Gen. William H. Draper reported that foreign aid was being undercut by world population growth.

The inauguration of John F. Kennedy. Kennedy's election worried Sanger. But Kennedy, a Catholic, gave family planning high priority in his administration.

she viewed as a critical policy decision.

So she challenged the president of the United States to a debate on the subject. President Eisenhower announced that world population problems were not the government's business and that world population control and family planning were beyond the limits of American intervention. Sanger in turn announced that the president's views should be straightened out and that she would be glad to participate in the process. There was no debate.

Because President Eisenhower suppressed the Draper Report, Sanger was worried when a Catholic, John F. Kennedy, ran for president. She even announced that she would leave the country if he were elected.

John Kennedy, however, refused to permit religion to interfere with interna-tional concerns. He pulled the Draper Report off the shelf of oblivion, and his administration began to change the policy of his predecessors. By 1963 the Council for the Planned Parenthood-World Federation was headed by two former United States presidents, Harry S Truman and Dwight D. Eisenhower. Eisenhower admitted that he had been mistaken about the world population movement. "I have come to believe," he said, "that the population explosion is the world's most critical problem."[73]

With this kind of high-level public support for birth control, Sanger's fight to gain recognition by the American government of its role in world population issues finally was won. She died in Tucson, Arizona, on September 6, 1966. She was a week short of her eighty-seventh birthday.

A Controversial Figure

When in 1957 Margaret Sanger was invited to appear on the Mike Wallace Show her appearance elicited many violent responses. The following editorial from the Catholic Evangelist *of September 17, 1957 is typical of the hundreds of letters sent to her in the aftermath of her appearance.*

"A graphic instance of the need of vigilance and prudent supervision of television programs was provided last night in The Mike Wallace Interview with Margaret Sanger. In permitting Wallace to give vent to his offensive sensationalism, the National Broadcasting Company and Philip Morris cigarettes, the sponsor of Wallace's program, pervert the aim of television as a medium of culture, education and entertainment.

Wallace, who claimed 'to explore the economic, moral and religious aspects of birth control' was the instrument whereby Mrs. Sanger, veteran proponent of barnyard ethics and race suicide, was given entrance into millions of decent homes to taint them with her evil philosophy of lust and animalist mating. If Margaret Sanger had her way, the ultimate result would be no audience for TV and no rising generations to 'Call for Philip Morris.'"

An Assessment

It is rare for a person to wage a lifelong crusade and to die with the knowledge that the crusade was a success. Margaret Sanger was one of those fortunate few. She brought the subject of contraception out of the darkness of Victorian prudishness and into the light of open and reasonable discussion.

She understood, and made many people in the United States understand, the physician's central role in the reproductive care of women. She also emphasized the need for women to make decisions about their own reproductive systems and the spacing of their families.

Under the influence of Margaret Sanger, sexuality as a subject of discussion generally ceased to be regarded as obscene. It became, instead, just one more aspect of human experience.

Sanger believed that contraception was not a morality issue and that women did not have to participate in maternity in order to live rich and full lives. For publicizing these views she is rightly considered one of the founders of the American women's movement.

Finally, Margaret Sanger was among the first to understand and publicize the relationship between population pressure and international conflict. What she saw in Germany and Japan in the 1920s and 1930s encouraged her to fight for international acceptance of birth control for the betterment of the planet. She urged its necessity to the League of Nations and later to the United Nations. And she fought her final and successful battle to provide an oral method of birth control that could be offered to the world's women, even in remote places far removed from the services of physicians and of clinics.

Honors poured in on Margaret Sanger in her old age. One in particular brought her singular pleasure. The emperor of Japan, for whose country she had worked so hard, extended a special greeting and honor shortly before her death. The emperor sent her a gold medal in appreciation of the work for birth control that she had done for his country. She was still wearing the medal over her nightgown when she died.

The day after her death, the *New York Times* called Margaret Sanger "one of history's great rebels and a monumental figure of the first half of the twentieth century."[74] She truly made a significant contribution to the United States and to the world.

Notes

Introduction

1. Lawrence Lader, *The Margaret Sanger Story*. Westport, CT: Geenwood Press, 1955.

Chapter 1: Beginnings and Stirrings

2. Lader, *The Margaret Sanger Story*.

3. Margaret Sanger, *An Autobiography*. New York: W. W. Norton and Company, 1938.

4. Sanger, *Autobiography*.

5. Margaret Sanger, *My Fight for Birth Control*. New York: Farrar and Rinehart, 1931.

6. Sanger, *Autobiography*.

7. Sanger, *Autobiography*.

Chapter 2: Women and Reproductive Choices

8. Emily Taft Douglas, *Margaret Sanger: Pioneer of the Future*. New York: Holt, Rinehart, and Winston, 1970.

9. David M. Kennedy, *Birth Control in America*. New Haven, CT: Yale University Press, 1970.

10. Kennedy, *Birth Control in America*.

11. Sanger, *My Fight for Birth Control*.

12. Sanger, *Autobiography*.

13. Madeline Gray, *Margaret Sanger*. New York: Richard Marek Publishers, 1979.

14. *The Woman Rebel*, March 1914.

15. Gray, *Margaret Sanger*.

16. Margaret Sanger, *Family Limitations*, 1914.

Chapter 3: Acquiring Knowledge to Start a Revolution

17. Margaret Sanger, *Pivot of Civilization*. London: Jonathan Cape, 1923.

18. Sanger, *Pivot of Civilization*.

19. Sanger, *Autobiography*.

20. Sanger, *My Fight for Birth Control*.

21. Douglas, *Margaret Sanger*.

22. Sanger, *Autobiography*.

23. Richard Allen Soloway, *Birth Control and the Population Question in England, 1877-1930*. Chapel Hill: University of North Carolina Press, 1982.

24. *The New York Globe*, February 1916.

Chapter 4: The Fight for Birth Control Clinics

25. Excerpt from an interview by reporter Kenneth W. Payne, 1916, which was part of a 1916 speech to the nation. Excerpted from Gray, *Margaret Sanger*.

26. Excerpt from same interview.

27. Excerpt from same interview.

28. *Birth Control Review*, February 1917.

29. Sanger, *Autobiography*.

30. Sanger, *My Fight for Birth Control*.

31. *St. Paul Dispatch,* January 1917, quoted in Gray, *Margaret Sanger*.

32. *Milwaukee Free Press*, January 1917, quoted in Gray, *Margaret Sanger*.

33. Margaret Sanger, *Women and the New Race*. New York: Truth Publishing Company, 1920.

34. Sanger, *Autobiography*.

35. Sanger, *My Fight for Birth Control*.

Chapter 5: Refining the Birth Control Movement

36. Kurt W. Back, *Family Planning and Population Control*. Boston: Twayne Publishers, 1989.

37. *The New York Times*, November 1922.

38. *New York Herald Tribune*, November 1922.

39. *New York Post*, November 1922.

40. Douglas, *Margaret Sanger*.

41. Sanger, *My Fight for Birth Control*.

42. Judge Harry Fisher, in *writ of mandamus*, 1923, quoted in Douglas, *Margaret Sanger*.

43. Lader, *The Margaret Sanger Story.*
44. Douglas, *Margaret Sanger.*
45. Kennedy, *Birth Control in America.*
46. Douglas, *Margaret Sanger.*
47. Douglas, *Margaret Sanger.*
48. Kennedy, *Birth Control in America.*
49. Gray, *Margaret Sanger.*

Chapter 6: Operating on a Federal Level

50. Gray, *Margaret Sanger.*
51. Sanger, *Autobiography.*
52. Sanger, *Autobiography.*
53. Lader, *The Margaret Sanger Story.*
54. Lader, *The Margaret Sanger Story.*
55. Lader, *The Margaret Sanger Story.*
56. Douglas, *Margaret Sanger.*
57. Lader, *The Margaret Sanger Story.*
58. Sanger, *Autobiography.*
59. Lader, *The Margaret Sanger Story.*
60. Gray, *Margaret Sanger.*

Chapter 7: Bigger Worlds and Other Fights

61. Sanger, *Autobiography.*
62. Lader, *The Margaret Sanger Story.*
63. Soloway, *Birth Control and the Population Question in England, 1877-1930.*
64. Lader, *The Margaret Sanger Story.*
65. Sanger, *Autobiography.*
66. Sanger, *My Fight for Birth Control.*
67. Gray, *Margaret Sanger.*
68. Douglas, *Margaret Sanger.*
69. Sanger, *My Fight for Birth Control.*
70. Sanger, *Autobiography.*

Chapter 8: Contributions

71. Angus McLaren, *A History of Contraception.* New York: W. W. Norton, 1990.
72. Back, *Family Planning and Population Control.*
73. Kennedy, *Birth Control in America.*
74. *New York Times,* September 7, 1966.

Bibliography

Heywood Broun and Margaret Leech, *Anthony Comstock*. New York: Boni, 1927. A fairly balanced treatment of a man considered by many to be a fanatic. Comstock's background motivated his concern to maintain public morals.

Emily Taft Douglas, *Margaret Sanger: Pioneer of the Future*. New York: Holt, Rinehart, and Winston, 1970. A relatively short, very favorable biography of Sanger. It contains many interesting pictures and some useful quotations.

Madeline Gray, *Margaret Sanger*. New York: Richard Marek Publishers, 1979. Extremely interesting to readers who wish to get an understanding of the correspondence between Sanger and many of her friends and admirers. It contains long extracts from that correspondence, much of it highly personal. The author also dedicates a good deal of the book to the personal life of Sanger.

David M. Kennedy, *Birth Control in America*. New Haven, CT: Yale University Press, 1970. A recent book that presents a balanced view of its subject.

Lawrence Lader, *The Margaret Sanger Story*. Westport, CT: Greenwood Press, 1955. A relatively easy to read, older account of Sanger which was published several years before Sanger's death.

William Manchester, *Winston Spencer Churchill: The Last Lion*. New York: Dell, 1989. Manchester's work provides a tremendous amount of background information regarding the social customs of the Victorian era.

Angus McLaren, *A History of Contraception*. New York: Norton, 1990. Gives a history of early civilizations and how they dealt with the problem of unwanted pregnancy.

Margaret Sanger, *An Autobiography*. New York: W. W. Norton and Company, 1938. Contains just the information that Sanger believed would be useful for the cause of the birth control movement. It contains much disinformation which must be corrected through research and the evaluation of other data.

——————————, *Happiness in Marriage*. New York: Brentano, 1926. Useful as a piece of propaganda. Sanger wrote the book to appeal to an audience which wished to learn how married women could improve their relationships through self realization.

——————————, *Motherhood in Bondage*. New York: Brentano, 1928. Sanger wrote this book as a piece of propaganda. Her central theme—that motherhood should be the result of a conscious decision to bear children—is heavily emphasized.

——————————, *My Fight for Birth Control*. New York: Farrar and Rinehart, 1931. Like her autobiography, Sanger wrote this book to provide information and propaganda to be used by her followers and supporters. It has the tone of a strident newspaper, rather than a serious work of literature.

——————————, *Pivot of Civilization*. London: Jonathan Cape, 1923. Another didactic work that focuses on how controlling birth has been central to the lives of women throughout recorded time.

——————————, *Women and the New Race*. New York: Truth Publishing Company, 1920. Sanger sets forth her own views on the role of sex in the life of both married and unmarried women.

Richard Allen Soloway, *Birth Control and the Population Question in England, 1877-1930*. Chapel Hill: University of North Carolina Press, 1982. Useful information regarding the birth control movement in Great Britain. It enables the reader to gain an understanding of how the British and American movements for birth control both supported and detracted from one another.

Index

Picture Credits

About the Author

Deborah Bachrach was born and raised in New York City, where she received her undergraduate education. She earned a Ph.D. in history from the University of Minnesota. Dr. Bachrach has taught at the University of Minnesota as well as at St. Francis College, Joliet, Illinois, and Queens College, the City University of New York. In addition, she has worked for many years in the fields of medical research and public policy development.